The Essential 2023 Air Fryer Cookbook

2000 Day Tasty Delicious & Effortless Air Fryer Recipes That Anyone Can Cook at Home

Lisa E. Rabinowitz

All rights reserved worldwide.

No part of this book may be reproduced or transmitted in any form or by any means,

electronic or mechanical, including photo copying, recording or by any information storage and retrieval system, without written permission from the publisher, except for the inclusion of brief quotations in a review.

Warning-Disclaimer:

The purpose of this book is to educate and entertain. The author or publisher does not guarantee that anyone following the techniques, suggestions, tips, ideas, or strategies will become successful. The author and publisher shall have neither liability or responsibility to anyone with respect to any loss or damage caused, or alleged to be caused, directly or indirectly by the information contained in this book.

CONTENTS

Breakfast & Snacks And Fries Recipes 10

Mexican Breakfast Burritos 10

Breakfast Sausage Burgers 10

Bocconcini Balls 11

Easy Cheesy Scrambled Eggs 11

Apple Crisps 12

Hard Boiled Eggs Air Fryer Style 12

Toad In The Hole, Breakfast Style 13

Crunchy Mexican Breakfast Wrap 13

Healthy Breakfast Bagels 14

Potato Fries 14

European Pancakes 15

Breakfast Eggs & Spinach 15

French Toast 16

Meaty Egg Cups 16

Baba Ganoush 17

Egg & Bacon Breakfast Cups 17

Healthy Stuffed Peppers 18

Polenta Fries 18

Wholegrain Pitta Chips 19

Easy Omelette 19

Blanket Breakfast Eggs 20

Oozing Baked Eggs 20

French Toast Slices 21

Sauces & Snack And Appetiser Recipes 22

Italian Rice Balls 22

Peppers With Aioli Dip 23

Spicy Peanuts	23
Cheese Wontons	24
Jalapeño Poppers	24
Mozzarella Sticks	25
Pepperoni Bread	25
Stuffed Mushrooms	26
Tasty Pumpkin Seeds	26
Onion Pakoda	27
Spicy Chickpeas	27
Corn Nuts	28
Cheesy Taco Crescents	28
Pasta Chips	29
weet Potato Crisps	29
Mac & Cheese Bites	29
Snack Style Falafel	30
Chicken & Bacon Parcels	30
Pretzel Bites	31
Salt And Vinegar Chickpeas	31
Air-fried Pickles	32
Waffle Fries	32
Popcorn Tofu	33
Vegetarian & Vegan Recipes	**34**
Sticky Tofu With Cauliflower Rice	34
Whole Wheat Pizza	34
Artichoke Pasta	35
Ratatouille	35
Roast Vegetables	36
Onion Dumplings	36

Courgette Burgers 37

Rainbow Vegetables 37

Jackfruit Taquitos 38

Potato Gratin 38

Air-fried Artichoke Hearts 39

Spring Ratatouille 39

Shakshuka 40

Macaroni & Cheese Quiche 41

Gnocchi Caprese 41

Lentil Burgers 42

Saganaki 42

Mini Quiche 43

Veggie Bakes 43

Goat's Cheese Tartlets 44

Vegan Meatballs 44

Spinach And Feta Croissants 45

Paneer Tikka 45

Beef & Lamb And Pork Recipes 46

Sweet And Sticky Ribs 46

Beef Kebobs 46

Mongolian Beef 47

Steak And Mushrooms 47

Tahini Beef Bites 48

Pork Schnitzel 48

Buttermilk Pork Chops 49

Hamburgers With Feta 49

Carne Asada Chips 50

Steak Fajitas 50

Lamb Burgers 51

Steak Dinner 51

Roast Beef 52

Salt And Pepper Belly Pork 52

German Rouladen 52

Italian Meatballs 53

Honey & Mustard Meatballs 53

Pork Taquitos 54

Meatballs In Tomato Sauce 54

Pulled Pork, Bacon, And Cheese Sliders 55

Breaded Pork Chops 55

Vegetable & Beef Frittata 56

Chinese Chilli Beef 56

Poultry Recipes 57

Air Fryer Chicken Thigh Schnitzel 57

Air Fryer Bbq Chicken 57

Chicken & Potatoes 58

Pepper & Lemon Chicken Wings 58

Turkey Cutlets In Mushroom Sauce 59

Chicken And Wheat Stir Fry 59

Cheddar & Bbq Stuffed Chicken 60

Crispy Cornish Hen 60

Turkey And Mushroom Burgers 61

Chicken Parmesan With Marinara Sauce 61

Smoky Chicken Breast 62

Spicy Chicken Wing Drummettes 62

Nashville Chicken 63

Chicken Tikka Masala 64

Chicken Milanese 64

Quick Chicken Nuggets 65

Chicken Kiev 65

Air Fried Maple Chicken Thighs 66

Cornflake Chicken Nuggets 66

Buffalo Wings 67

Chicken Jalfrezi 67

Pizza Chicken Nuggets 68

Satay Chicken Skewers 68

Fish & Seafood Recipes 69

Air Fried Scallops 69

Copycat Fish Fingers 69

Fish In Foil 70

Cajun Shrimp Boil 70

Parmesan-coated Fish Fingers 71

Mahi Fish Tacos 71

Extra Crispy Popcorn Shrimp 72

Fish In Parchment Paper 72

Thai Fish Cakes 73

Shrimp With Yum Yum Sauce 73

Salt & Pepper Calamari 74

Fish Taco Cauliflower Rice Bowls 74

Store-cupboard Fishcakes 75

Gluten Free Honey And Garlic Shrimp 75

Chilli Lime Tilapia 76

Garlic Tilapia 76

Honey Sriracha Salmon 77

Ranch Style Fish Fillets 77

Cajun Prawn Skewers 78

Air Fryer Mussels 78

Crunchy Fish 79

Cod Nuggets 79

Thai-style Tuna Fishcakes 80

Side Dishes Recipes 81

Potato Wedges With Rosemary 81

Cheesy Garlic Asparagus 81

Aubergine Parmesan 82

Yorkshire Puddings 82

Orange Tofu 83

Super Easy Fries 83

Shishito Peppers 84

Potato Wedges 84

Asparagus Spears 85

Zingy Roasted Carrots 85

Butternut Squash Fries 85

Celery Root Fries 86

Orange Sesame Cauliflower 86

Cauliflower With Hot Sauce And Blue Cheese Sauce 87

Honey Roasted Parsnips 87

Whole Sweet Potatoes 88

Crispy Sweet & Spicy Cauliflower 88

Crispy Broccoli 89

Ricotta Stuffed Aubergine 89

Alternative Stuffed Potatoes 90

Mediterranean Vegetables 90

Crispy Cinnamon French Toast 91

Air Fryer Eggy Bread 91

Desserts Recipes 92

Strawberry Danish 92

Thai Fried Bananas 92

Cinnamon-maple Pineapple Kebabs 93

Cinnamon Biscuit Bites 93

Brazilian Pineapple 94

Chocolate Mug Cake 94

Chocolate Cake 95

White Chocolate And Raspberry Loaf 95

Peach Pies(1) 96

Grilled Ginger & Coconut Pineapple Rings 96

Peanut Butter & Chocolate Baked Oats 97

Chonut Holes 97

Apple And Cinnamon Puff Pastry Pies 98

Banana And Nutella Sandwich 98

Pistachio Brownies 99

New York Cheesecake 99

Milk And White Chocolate Chip Air Fryer Donuts With Frosting 100

Pop Tarts 101

Banana Bread 101

Banana Cake 102

Butter Cake 102

Breakfast Muffins 103

White Chocolate Pudding 103

RECIPES INDEX 104

Breakfast & Snacks And Fries Recipes

Mexican Breakfast Burritos

Servings: 6
Cooking Time:xx
Ingredients:
- 6 scrambled eggs
- 6 medium tortillas
- Half a minced red pepper
- 8 sausages, cut into cubes and browned
- 4 pieces of bacon, pre-cooked and cut into pieces
- 65g grated cheese of your choice
- A small amount of olive oil for cooking

Directions:
1. Into a regular mixing bowl, combine the eggs, bell pepper, bacon pieces, the cheese, and the browned sausage, giving everything a good stir
2. Take your first tortilla and place half a cup of the mixture into the middle, folding up the top and bottom and rolling closed
3. Repeat until all your tortillas have been used
4. Arrange the burritos into the bottom of your fryer and spray with a little oil
5. Cook the burritos at 170°C for 5 minutes

Breakfast Sausage Burgers

Servings: 2
Cooking Time:xx
Ingredients:
- 8 links of your favourite sausage
- Salt and pepper to taste

Directions:
1. Remove the sausage from the skins and use a fork to create a smooth mixture
2. Season to your liking
3. Shape the sausage mixture into burgers or patties
4. Preheat your air fryer to 260°C
5. Arrange the burgers in the fryer, so they are not touching each other
6. Cook for 8 minutes
7. Serve still warm

Bocconcini Balls

Servings: 2
Cooking Time:xx
Ingredients:

- 70 g/½ cup plus ½ tablespoon plain/all-purpose flour (gluten-free if you wish)
- 1 egg, beaten
- 70 g/1 cup dried breadcrumbs (gluten-free if you wish; see page 9)
- 10 bocconcini

Directions:
1. Preheat the air-fryer to 200°C/400°F.
2. Place the flour, egg and breadcrumbs on 3 separate plates. Dip each bocconcini ball first in the flour to coat, then the egg, shaking off any excess before rolling in the breadcrumbs.
3. Add the breaded bocconcini to the preheated air-fryer and air-fry for 5 minutes (no need to turn them during cooking). Serve immediately.

Easy Cheesy Scrambled Eggs

Servings: 1
Cooking Time:xx
Ingredients:

- 1 tbsp butter
- 2 eggs
- 100g grated cheese
- 2 tbsp milk
- Salt and pepper for seasoning

Directions:
1. Add the butter inside the air fryer pan and cook at 220°C until the butter has melted
2. Add the eggs and milk to a bowl and combine, seasoning to your liking
3. Pour the eggs into the butter panned cook for 3 minutes, stirring around lightly to scramble
4. Add the cheese and cook for another 2 more minutes

Apple Crisps

Servings: 2
Cooking Time:xx
Ingredients:
- 2 apples, chopped
- 1 tsp cinnamon
- 2 tbsp brown sugar
- 1 tsp lemon juice
- 2.5 tbsp plain flour
- 3 tbsp oats
- 2 tbsp cold butter
- Pinch of salt

Directions:
1. Preheat the air fryer to 260°C
2. Take a 5" baking dish and crease
3. Take a large bowl and combine the apples with the sugar, cinnamon and lemon juice
4. Add the mixture to the baking dish and cover with aluminium foil
5. Place in the air fryer and cook for 15 minutes
6. Open the lid and cook for another 5 minutes
7. Combine the rest of the ingredients in a food processor, until a crumble-type mixture occurs
8. Add over the top of the cooked apples
9. Cook with the lid open for another 5 minutes
10. Allow to cool a little before serving

Hard Boiled Eggs Air Fryer Style

Servings: 2
Cooking Time:xx
Ingredients:
- 4 large eggs
- 1 tsp cayenne pepper
- Salt and pepper for seasoning

Directions:
1. Preheat the air fryer to 220°C
2. Take a wire rack and place inside the air fryer
3. Lay the eggs on the rack
4. Cook for between 15-17 minutes, depending upon how you like your eggs
5. Remove from the fryer and place in a bowl of cold water for around 5 minutes
6. Peel and season with the cayenne and the salt and pepper

Toad In The Hole, Breakfast Style

Servings: 4
Cooking Time:xx
Ingredients:
- 1 sheet of puff pastry (defrosted)
- 4 eggs
- 4 tbsp grated cheese (cheddar works well)
- 4 slices of cooked ham, cut into pieces
- Chopped fresh herbs of your choice

Directions:
1. Preheat your air fryer to 200°C
2. Take your pastry sheet and place it on a flat surface, cutting it into four pieces
3. Take two of the pastry sheets and place them inside your fryer, cooking for up to 8 minutes, until done
4. Remove the pastry and flatten the centre down with a spoon, to form a deep hole
5. Add a tablespoon of the cheese and a tablespoon of the ham into the hole
6. Crack one egg into the hole
7. Return the pastry to the air fryer and cook for another 6 minutes, or until the egg is done as you like it
8. Remove and allow to cool
9. Repeat the process with the rest of the pastry remaining
10. Sprinkle fresh herbs on top and serve

Crunchy Mexican Breakfast Wrap

Servings: 2
Cooking Time:xx
Ingredients:
- 2 large tortillas
- 2 corn tortillas
- 1 sliced jalapeño pepper
- 4 tbsp ranchero sauce
- 1 sliced avocado
- 25g cooked pinto beans

Directions:
1. Take each of your large tortillas and add the egg, jalapeño, sauce, the corn tortillas, the avocado and the pinto beans, in that order. If you want to add more sauce at this point, you can
2. Fold over your wrap to make sure that nothing escapes
3. Place each wrap into your fryer and cook at 190°C for 6 minutes
4. Remove your wraps and place in the oven, cooking for a further 5 minutes at 180°C, until crispy
5. Place each wrap into a frying pan and crisp a little more on a low heat, for a couple of minutes on each side

Healthy Breakfast Bagels

Servings: 2
Cooking Time:xx
Ingredients:
- 170g self raising flour
- 120ml plain yogurt
- 1 egg

Directions:
1. Take a large mixing bowl, combine the flour and the yogurt to create a dough
2. Cover a flat surface with a little extra flour and set the dough down
3. Create four separate and even balls
4. Roll each ball out into a rope shape and form a bagel with each
5. Take a small mixing bowl and whisk the egg
6. Brush the egg over the top of the bagel
7. Arrange the bagels inside your fryer evenly
8. Cook at 170°C for 10 minutes
9. Allow to cool before serving

Potato Fries

Servings: 2
Cooking Time:xx
Ingredients:
- 2 large potatoes (baking potato size)
- 1 teaspoon olive oil
- salt

Directions:
1. Peel the potatoes and slice into fries about 5 x 1.5cm/¾ x ¾ in. by the length of the potato. Submerge the fries in a bowl of cold water and place in the fridge for about 10 minutes.
2. Meanwhile, preheat the air-fryer to 160°C/325°F.
3. Drain the fries thoroughly, then toss in the oil and season. Tip into the preheated air-fryer in a single layer (you may need to cook them in two batches, depending on the size of your air-fryer). Air-fry for 15 minutes, tossing once during cooking by shaking the air-fryer drawer, then increase the temperature of the air-fryer to 200°C/400°F and cook for a further 3 minutes. Serve immediately.

European Pancakes

Servings: 5
Cooking Time:xx

Ingredients:
- 3 large eggs
- 130g flour
- 140ml whole milk
- 2 tbsp unsweetened apple sauce
- A pinch of salt

Directions:
1. Set your fryer to 200°C and add five ramekins inside to heat up
2. Place all your ingredients inside a blender to combine
3. Spray the ramekins with a little cooking spray
4. Pour the batter into the ramekins carefully
5. Fry for between 6-8 minutes, depending on your preference
6. Serve with your favourite toppings

Breakfast Eggs & Spinach

Servings: 4
Cooking Time:xx

Ingredients:
- 500g wilted, fresh spinach
- 200g sliced deli ham
- 1 tbsp olive oil
- 4 eggs
- 4 tsp milk
- Salt and pepper to taste
- 1 tbsp butter for cooking

Directions:
1. Preheat your air fryer to 180°C
2. You will need 4 small ramekin dishes, coated with a little butter
3. Arrange the wilted spinach, ham, 1 teaspoon of milk and 1 egg into each ramekin and season with a little salt and pepper
4. Place in the fryer 15 to 20 minutes, until the egg is cooked to your liking
5. Allow to cool before serving

French Toast

Servings: 2
Cooking Time:xx
Ingredients:
- 2 beaten eggs
- 2 tbsp softened butter
- 4 slices of sandwich bread
- 1 tsp cinnamon
- 1 tsp nutmeg
- 1 tsp ground cloves
- 1 tsp maple syrup

Directions:
1. Preheat your fryer to 180°C
2. Take a bowl and add the eggs, salt, cinnamon, nutmeg, and cloves, combining well
3. Take your bread and butter each side, cutting into strips
4. Dip the bread slices into the egg mixture
5. Arrange each slice into the basket of your fryer
6. Cook for 2 minutes
7. Take the basket out and spray with a little cooking spray
8. Turn over the slices and place back into the fryer
9. Cook for 4 minutes
10. Remove and serve with maple syrup

Meaty Egg Cups

Servings: 4
Cooking Time:xx
Ingredients:
- 8 slices of toasted sandwich bread
- 2 slices of ham
- 4 eggs
- Salt and pepper to taste
- Butter for greasing

Directions:
1. Take 4 ramekins and grease the insides with a little butter
2. Flatten the slices of toast with a rolling pin and arrange inside the ramekins - two in each
3. Line the inside of each ramekin with a slice of ham
4. Crack one egg into each ramekin
5. Season with a little salt and pepper
6. Place the ramekins into the air fryer and cook at 160°C for 15 minutes
7. Remove from the fryer and wait to cool just slightly
8. Remove and serve

Baba Ganoush

Servings: 4
Cooking Time:xx
Ingredients:
- 1 large aubergine/eggplant, sliced in half lengthways
- ½ teaspoon salt
- 5 tablespoons olive oil
- 1 bulb garlic
- 30 g/2 tablespoons tahini or nut butter
- 2 tablespoons freshly squeezed lemon juice
- ½ teaspoon ground cumin
- ¼ teaspoon smoked paprika
- salt and freshly ground black pepper
- 3 tablespoons freshly chopped flat-leaf parsley

Directions:
1. Preheat the air-fryer to 200°C/400°F.
2. Lay the aubergine/eggplant halves cut side up. Sprinkle over the salt, then drizzle over 1 tablespoon of oil. Cut the top off the garlic bulb, brush the exposed cloves with a little olive oil, then wrap in foil. Place the aubergine/eggplant and foil-wrapped garlic in the preheated air-fryer and air-fry for 15–20 minutes until the inside of the aubergine is soft and buttery in texture.
3. Scoop the flesh of the aubergine into a bowl. Squeeze out about 1 tablespoon of the cooked garlic and add to the bowl with the remaining 4 tablespoons of olive oil, the tahini/nut butter, lemon juice, spices and salt and pepper to taste. Mix well and serve with fresh flat-leaf parsley sprinkled over.

Egg & Bacon Breakfast Cups

Servings: 8
Cooking Time:xx
Ingredients:
- 6 eggs
- 1 chopped red pepper
- 1 chopped green pepper
- 1 chopped yellow pepper
- 2 tbsp double cream
- 50g chopped spinach
- 50g grated cheddar cheese
- 50g grated mozzarella cheese
- 3 slices of cooked bacon, crumbled into pieces

Directions:
1. Take a large mixing bowl and crack the eggs
2. Add the cream and season with a little salt and pepper, combining everything well
3. Add the peppers, spinach, onions, both cheeses, and the crumbled bacon, combining everything once more
4. You will need silicone moulds or cups for this part, and you should pour equal amounts of the mixture into 8 cups
5. Cook at 150°C for around 12 or 15 minutes, until the eggs are cooked properly

Healthy Stuffed Peppers

Servings: 2
Cooking Time:xx
Ingredients:
- 1 large bell pepper, deseeded and cut into halves
- 1 tsp olive oil
- 4 large eggs
- Salt and pepper to taste

Directions:
1. Take your peppers and rub a little olive oil on the edges
2. Into each pepper, crack one egg and season with salt and pepper
3. You will need to insert a trivet into your air fryer to hold the peppers, and then arrange the peppers evenly
4. Set your fryer to 200°C and cook for 13 minutes
5. Once cooked, remove and serve with a little more seasoning, if required

Polenta Fries

Servings: 6
Cooking Time:xx
Ingredients:
- 800 ml/scant 3½ cups water
- 1½ vegetable stock cubes
- ¾ teaspoon dried oregano
- ¾ teaspoon freshly ground black pepper
- 200 g/1⅓ cups quick-cook polenta/cornmeal
- 2 teaspoons olive oil
- 55 g/6 tablespoons plain/all-purpose flour (gluten-free if you wish)
- garlic mayonnaise, to serve

Directions:
1. Bring the water and stock cubes to the boil in a saucepan with the oregano and black pepper. Stir in the polenta/cornmeal and continue to stir until the mixture becomes significantly more solid and is hard to stir – this should take about 5–6 minutes.
2. Grease a 15 x 15-cm/6 x 6-in. baking pan with some of the olive oil. Tip the polenta into the baking pan, smoothing down with the back of a wet spoon. Leave to cool at room temperature for about 30 minutes, then pop into the fridge for at least an hour.
3. Remove the polenta from the fridge and carefully tip out onto a chopping board. Slice the polenta into fingers 7.5 x 1 x 2 cm/3 x ½ x ¾ in. Roll the polenta fingers in the flour, then spray or drizzle the remaining olive oil over the fingers.
4. Preheat the air-fryer to 200°C/400°F.
5. Lay the fingers apart from one another in a single layer in the preheated air-fryer (you may need to cook these in batches, depending on the size of your air-fryer). Air-fry for 9 minutes, turning once halfway through cooking. Serve immediately with garlic mayonnaise.

Wholegrain Pitta Chips

Servings: 2
Cooking Time:xx
Ingredients:
- 2 round wholegrain pittas, chopped into quarters
- 1 teaspoon olive oil
- ½ teaspoon garlic salt

Directions:
1. Preheat the air-fryer to 180°C/350°F.
2. Spray or brush each pitta quarter with olive oil and sprinkle with garlic salt. Place in the preheated air-fryer and air-fry for 4 minutes, turning halfway through cooking. Serve immediately.

Easy Omelette

Servings: 1
Cooking Time:xx
Ingredients:
- 50ml milk
- 2 eggs
- 60g grated cheese, any you like
- Any garnishes you like, such as mushrooms, peppers, etc.

Directions:
1. Take a small mixing bowl and crack the eggs inside, whisking with the milk
2. Add the salt and garnishes and combine again
3. Grease a 6x3" pan and pour the mixture inside
4. Arrange the pan inside the air fryer basket
5. Cook at 170°C for 10 minutes
6. At the halfway point, sprinkle the cheese on top
7. Loosen the edges with a spatula before serving

Blanket Breakfast Eggs

Servings: 2
Cooking Time:xx
Ingredients:

- 2 eggs
- 2 slices of sandwich bread
- Olive oil spray
- Salt and pepper to taste

Directions:

1. Preheat your air fryer to 190°C and spray with a little oil
2. Meanwhile, take your bread and cut a hole into the middle of each piece
3. Place one slice inside your fryer and crack one egg into the middle
4. Season with a little salt and pepper
5. Cook for 5 minutes, before turning over and cooking for a further 2 minutes
6. Remove the first slice and repeat the process with the remaining slice of bread and egg

Oozing Baked Eggs

Servings: 2
Cooking Time:xx
Ingredients:

- 4 eggs
- 140g smoked gouda cheese, cut into small pieces
- Salt and pepper to taste

Directions:

1. You will need two ramekin dishes and spray each one before using
2. Crack two eggs into each ramekin dish
3. Add half of the Gouda cheese to each dish
4. Season and place into the air fryer
5. Cook at 350°C for 15 minutes, until the eggs are cooked as you like them

French Toast Slices

Servings: 1
Cooking Time:xx

Ingredients:

- 2 eggs
- 5 slices sandwich bread
- 100ml milk
- 2 tbsp flour
- 3 tbsp sugar
- 1 tsp ground cinnamon
- 1/2 tsp vanilla extract
- Pinch of salt

Directions:

1. Preheat your air fryer to 220°C
2. Take your bread and cut it into three pieces of the same size
3. Take a mixing bowl and combine the other ingredients until smooth
4. Dip the bread into the mixture, coating evenly
5. Take a piece of parchment paper and lay it inside the air fryer
6. Arrange the bread on the parchment paper in one layer
7. Cook for 5 minutes
8. Turn and cook for another 5 minutes

Sauces & Snack And Appetiser Recipes

Italian Rice Balls

Servings: 2
Cooking Time:xx

Ingredients:
- 400g cooked rice
- 25g breadcrumbs, plus an extra 200g for breading
- 2 tbsp flour, plus an extra 2 tbsp for breading
- 1 tbsp cornstarch, plus an extra 3 tbsp for breading
- 1 chopped bell pepper
- 1 chopped onion
- 2 tbsp olive oil
- 1 tsp red chilli flakes
- 5 chopped mozzarella cheese sticks
- A little water for the breading
- Salt and pepper for seasoning

Directions:
1. Place the cooked rice into a bowl and mash with a fork. Place to one side
2. Take a saucepan and add the oil, salting the onion and peppers until they're both soft
3. Add the chilli flakes and a little salt and combine
4. Add the mixture to the mashed rice and combine
5. Add the 2 tbsp flour and 1 tbsp cornstarch, along with the 25g breadcrumbs and combine well
6. Use your hands to create balls with the mixture
7. Stuff a piece of the mozzarella inside the balls and form around it
8. Take a bowl and add the rest of the flour, corn starch and a little seasoning, with a small amount of water to create a thick batter
9. Take another bowl and add the rest of the breadcrumbs
10. Dip each rice ball into the batter and then the breadcrumbs
11. Preheat the air fryer to 220ºC
12. Cook for 6 minutes, before shaking and cooking for another 6 minutes

Peppers With Aioli Dip

Servings: 4
Cooking Time:xx
Ingredients:
- 250g shishito peppers
- 2 tsp avocado oil
- 5 tbsp mayonnaise
- 2 tbsp lemon juice
- 1 minced clove of garlic
- 1 tbsp chopped parsley
- Salt and pepper for seasoning

Directions:
1. Take a medium bowl and combine the mayonnaise with the lemon juice, garlic, parsley and seasoning and create a smooth dip
2. Preheat the air fryer to 220°C
3. Toss the peppers in the oil and add to the air fryer
4. Cook for 4 minutes, until the peppers are soft and blistered on the outside
5. Remove and serve with the dip

Spicy Peanuts

Servings: 8
Cooking Time:xx
Ingredients:
- 2 tbsp olive oil
- 3 tbsp seafood seasoning
- ½ tsp cayenne
- 300g raw peanuts
- Salt to taste

Directions:
1. Preheat the air fryer to 160°C
2. Whisk together ingredients in a bowl and stir in the peanuts
3. Add to air fryer and cook for 10 minutes, shake then cook for a further 10 minutes
4. Sprinkle with salt and cook for another 5 minutes

Cheese Wontons

Servings: 8
Cooking Time:xx
Ingredients:
- 8 wonton wrappers
- 1 carton pimento cheese
- Small dish of water
- Cooking spray

Directions:
1. Place one tsp of cheese in the middle of each wonton wrapper
2. Brush the edges of each wonton wrapper with water
3. Fold over to create a triangle and seal
4. Heat the air fryer to 190°C
5. Spray the wontons with cooking spray
6. Place in the air fryer and cook for 3 minutes
7. Turnover and cook for a further 3 minutes

Jalapeño Poppers

Servings: 2
Cooking Time:xx
Ingredients:
- 10 jalapeños, halved and deseeded
- 100g cream cheese
- 50g parsley
- 150g breadcrumbs

Directions:
1. Mix 1/2 the breadcrumbs with the cream cheese
2. Add the parsley
3. Stuff the peppers with the cream cheese mix
4. Top the peppers with the remaining breadcrumbs
5. Heat the air fryer to 185°C
6. Place in the air fryer and cook for 6-8 minutes

Mozzarella Sticks

Servings: 4
Cooking Time:xx

Ingredients:
- 60ml water
- 50g flour
- 5 tbsp cornstarch
- 1 tbsp cornmeal
- 1 tsp garlic powder
- ½ tsp salt
- 100g breadcrumbs
- ½ tsp pepper
- ½ tsp parsley
- ½ tsp onion powder
- ¼ tsp oregano
- ½ tsp basil
- 200g mozzarella cut into ½ inch strips

Directions:
1. Mix water, flour, cornstarch, cornmeal, garlic powder and salt in a bowl
2. Stir breadcrumbs, pepper, parsley, onion powder, oregano and basil together in another bowl
3. Dip the mozzarella sticks in the batter then coat in the breadcrumbs
4. Heat the air fryer to 200°C
5. Cook for 6 minutes turn and cook for another 6 minutes

Pepperoni Bread

Servings: 4
Cooking Time:xx

Ingredients:
- Cooking spray
- 400g pizza dough
- 200g pepperoni
- 1 tbsp dried oregano
- Ground pepper to taste
- Garlic salt to taste
- 1 tsp melted butter
- 1 tsp grated parmesan
- 50g grated mozzarella

Directions:
1. Line a baking tin with 2 inch sides with foil to fit in the air fryer
2. Spray with cooking spray
3. Preheat the air fryer to 200°C
4. Roll the pizza dough into 1 inch balls and line the baking tin
5. Sprinkle with pepperoni, oregano, pepper and garlic salt
6. Brush with melted butter and sprinkle with parmesan
7. Place in the air fryer and cook for 15 minutes
8. Sprinkle with mozzarella and cook for another 2 minutes

Stuffed Mushrooms

Servings: 24
Cooking Time:xx
Ingredients:
- 24 mushrooms
- ½ pepper, sliced
- ½ diced onion
- 1 small carrot, diced
- 200g grated cheese
- 2 slices bacon, diced
- 100g sour cream

Directions:
1. Place the mushroom stems, pepper, onion, carrot and bacon in a pan and cook for about 5 minutes
2. Stir in cheese and sour cream, cook until well combined
3. Heat the air fryer to 175°C
4. Add stuffing to each of the mushrooms
5. Place in the air fryer and cook for 8 minutes

Tasty Pumpkin Seeds

Servings: 2
Cooking Time:xx
Ingredients:
- 1 ¾ cups pumpkin seeds
- 2 tsp avocado oil
- 1 tsp paprika
- 1 tsp salt

Directions:
1. Preheat air fryer to 180°C
2. Add all ingredients to a bowl and mix well
3. Place in the air fryer and cook for 35 minutes shaking frequently

Onion Pakoda

Servings: 2
Cooking Time:xx

Ingredients:
- 200g gram flour
- 2 onions, thinly sliced
- 1 tbsp crushed coriander seeds
- 1 tsp chilli powder
- ¾ tsp salt
- ¼ tsp turmeric
- ¼ tsp baking soda

Directions:
1. Mix all the ingredients together in a large bowl
2. Make bite sized pakodas
3. Heat the air fryer to 200°C
4. Line the air fryer with foil
5. Place the pakoda in the air fryer and cook for 5 minutes
6. Turn over and cook for a further 5 minutes

Spicy Chickpeas

Servings: 4
Cooking Time:xx

Ingredients:
- 1 can chickpeas
- 1 tbsp yeast
- 1 tbsp olive oil
- 1 tsp paprika
- 1 tsp garlic powder
- ½ tsp salt
- Pinch cumin

Directions:
1. Preheat air fryer to 180°C
2. Combine all ingredients
3. Add to the air fryer and cook for 22 minutes tossing every 4 minutes until cooked

Corn Nuts

Servings: 8
Cooking Time:xx
Ingredients:
- 1 giant white corn
- 3 tbsp vegetable oil
- 2 tsp salt

Directions:
1. Place the corn in a large bowl, cover with water and sit for 8 hours
2. Drain, pat dry and air dry for 20 minutes
3. Preheat the air fryer to 200°C
4. Place in a bowl and coat with oil and salt
5. Cook in the air fryer for 10 minutes shake then cook for a further 10 minutes

Cheesy Taco Crescents

Servings: 8
Cooking Time:xx
Ingredients:
- 1 can Pillsbury crescent sheets, or alternative
- 4 Monterey Jack cheese sticks
- 150g browned minced beef
- ½ pack taco seasoning mix

Directions:
1. Preheat the air fryer to 200°C
2. Combine the minced beef and the taco seasoning, warm in the microwave for about 2 minutes
3. Cut the crescent sheets into 8 equal squares
4. Cut the cheese sticks in half
5. Add half a cheese stick to each square, and 2 tablespoons of mince
6. Roll up the dough and pinch at the ends to seal
7. Place in the air fryer and cook for 5 minutes
8. Turnover and cook for another 3 minutes

Pasta Chips

Servings: 2
Cooking Time:xx
Ingredients:
- 300g dry pasta bows
- 1 tbsp olive oil
- 1 tbsp nutritional yeast
- 1½ tsp Italian seasoning
- ½ tsp salt

Directions:
1. Cook the pasta for half the time stated on the packet
2. Drain and mix with the oil, yeast, seasoning and salt
3. Place in the air fryer and cook at 200°C for 5 minutes shake and cook for a further 3 minutes until crunchy

weet Potato Crisps

Servings: 4
Cooking Time:xx
Ingredients:
- 1 sweet potato, peeled and thinly sliced
- 2 tbsp oil
- ¼ tsp salt
- ¼ tsp pepper
- 1 tsp chopped rosemary
- Cooking spray

Directions:
1. Place all ingredients in a bowl and mix well
2. Place in the air fryer and cook at 175°C for about 15 minutes until crispy

Mac & Cheese Bites

Servings: 14
Cooking Time:xx
Ingredients:
- 200g mac and cheese
- 2 eggs
- 200g panko breadcrumbs
- Cooking spray

Directions:
1. Place drops of mac and cheese on parchment paper and freeze for 1 hour
2. Beat the eggs in a bowl, add the breadcrumbs to another bowl
3. Dip the mac and cheese balls in the egg then into the breadcrumbs
4. Heat the air fryer to 190°C
5. Place in the air fryer, spray with cooking spray and cook for 15 minutes

Snack Style Falafel

Servings: 15
Cooking Time:xx
Ingredients:
- 150g dry garbanzo beans
- 300g coriander
- 75g flat leaf parsley
- 1 red onion, quartered
- 1 clove garlic
- 2 tbsp chickpea flour
- Cooking spray
- 1 tbsp cumin
- 1 tbsp coriander
- 1 tbsp sriracha
- ½ tsp baking powder
- Salt and pepper to taste
- ¼ tsp baking soda

Directions:
1. Add all ingredients apart from the baking soda and baking powder to a food processor and blend well
2. Cover and rest for 1 hour
3. Heat air fryer to 190°C
4. Add baking powder and baking soda to mix and combine
5. Form mix into 15 equal balls
6. Spray air fryer with cooking spray
7. Add to air fryer and cook for 8-10 minutes

Chicken & Bacon Parcels

Servings: 4
Cooking Time:xx
Ingredients:
- 2 chicken breasts, boneless and skinless
- 200ml BBQ sauce
- 7 slices of bacon, cut lengthwise into halves
- 2 tbsp brown sugar

Directions:
1. Preheat the air fryer to 220°C
2. Cut the chicken into strips, you should have 7 in total
3. Wrap two strips of the bacon around each piece of chicken
4. Brush the BBQ sauce over the top and sprinkle with the brown sugar
5. Place the chicken into the basket and cook for 5 minutes
6. Turn the chicken over and cook for another 5 minutes

Pretzel Bites

Servings: 2
Cooking Time:xx
Ingredients:
- 650g flour
- 2.5 tsp active dry yeast
- 260ml hot water
- 1 tsp salt
- 4 tbsp melted butter
- 2 tbsp sugar

Directions:
1. Take a large bowl and add the flour, sugar and salt
2. Take another bowl and combine the hot water and yeast, stirring until the yeast has dissolved
3. Then, add the yeast mixture to the flour mixture and use your hands to combine
4. Knead for 2 minutes
5. Cover the bowl with a kitchen towel for around half an hour
6. Divide the dough into 6 pieces
7. Preheat the air fryer to 260°C
8. Take each section of dough and tear off a piece, rolling it in your hands to create a rope shape, that is around 1" in thickness
9. Cut into 2" strips
10. Place the small dough balls into the air fryer and leave a little space in-between
11. Cook for 6 minutes
12. Once cooked, remove and brush with melted butter and sprinkle salt on top

Salt And Vinegar Chickpeas

Servings: 5
Cooking Time:xx
Ingredients:
- 1 can chickpeas
- 100ml white vinegar
- 1 tbsp olive oil
- Salt to taste

Directions:
1. Combine chickpeas and vinegar in a pan, simmer remove from heat and stand for 30 minutes
2. Preheat the air fryer to 190°C
3. Drain chickpeas
4. Place chickpeas in the air fryer and cook for about 4 minutes
5. Pour chickpeas into an ovenproof bowl drizzle with oil, sprinkle with salt
6. Place bowl in the air fryer and cook for another 4 minutes

Air-fried Pickles

Servings: 4
Cooking Time:xx
Ingredients:
- 1/2 cup mayonnaise
- 2 tsp sriracha sauce
- 1 jar dill pickle slices
- 1 egg
- 2 tbsp milk
- 50g flour
- 50g cornmeal
- ½ tsp seasoned salt
- ¼ tsp paprika
- ¼ tsp garlic powder
- ⅛ tsp pepper
- Cooking spray

Directions:
1. Mix the mayo and sriracha together in a bowl and set aside
2. Heat the air fryer to 200°C
3. Drain the pickles and pat dry
4. Mix egg and milk together, in another bowl mix all the remaining ingredients
5. Dip the pickles in the egg mix then in the flour mix
6. Spray the air fryer with cooking spray
7. Cook for about 4 minutes until crispy

Waffle Fries

Servings: 4
Cooking Time:xx
Ingredients:
- 2 large potatoes, russet potatoes work best
- 1 tsp salt for seasoning
- Waffle cutter

Directions:
1. Peel the potatoes and slice using the waffle cutter. You can also use a mandolin cutter that has a blade
2. Transfer the potatoes to a bowl and season with the salt, coating evenly
3. Add to the air fryer and cook at 220°C for 15 minutes, shaking every so often

Popcorn Tofu

Servings: 4
Cooking Time:xx

Ingredients:

- 400g firm tofu
- 100g chickpea flour
- 100g oatmeal
- 2 tbsp yeast
- 150ml milk
- 400g breadcrumbs
- 1 tsp garlic powder
- 1 tsp onion powder
- 1 tbsp dijon mustard
- ½ tsp salt
- ½ tsp pepper
- 2 tbsp vegetable bouillon

Directions:

1. Rip the tofu into pieces. Place the breadcrumbs into a bowl, in another bowl mix the remaining ingredients
2. Dip the tofu into the batter mix and then dip into the breadcrumbs
3. Heat the air fryer to 175°C
4. Place the tofu in the air fryer and cook for 12 minutes shaking halfway through

Vegetarian & Vegan Recipes

Sticky Tofu With Cauliflower Rice

Servings:4
Cooking Time:20 Minutes
Ingredients:
- For the tofu:
- 1 x 180 g / 6 oz block firm tofu
- 2 tbsp soy sauce
- 1 onion, sliced
- 1 large carrot, peeled and thinly sliced
- For the cauliflower:
- 200 g / 7 oz cauliflower florets
- 2 tbsp soy sauce
- 1 tbsp sesame oil
- 2 cloves garlic, minced
- 100 g / 3.5 oz broccoli, chopped into small florets

Directions:
1. Preheat the air fryer to 190 °C / 370 °F and line the air fryer with parchment paper or grease it with olive oil.
2. Crumble the tofu into a bowl and mix in the soy sauce, and the sliced onion and carrot.
3. Cook the tofu and vegetables in the air fryer for 10 minutes.
4. Meanwhile, place the cauliflower florets into a blender and pulse until it forms a rice-like consistency.
5. Place the cauliflower rice in a bowl and mix in the soy sauce, sesame oil, minced garlic cloves, and broccoli florets until well combined. Transfer to the air fryer and cook for 10 minutes until hot and crispy.

Whole Wheat Pizza

Servings: 2
Cooking Time:xx
Ingredients:
- 100g marinara sauce
- 2 whole wheat pitta
- 200g baby spinach leaves
- 1 small plum tomato, sliced
- 1 clove garlic, sliced
- 400g grated cheese
- 50g shaved parmesan

Directions:
1. Preheat air fryer to 160ºC
2. Spread each of the pitta with marinara sauce
3. Sprinkle with cheese, top with spinach, plum tomato and garlic. Finish with parmesan shavings
4. Place in the air fryer and cook for about 4 mins cheese has melted

Artichoke Pasta

Servings: 2
Cooking Time:xx
Ingredients:
- 100g pasta
- 50g basil leaves
- 6 artichoke hearts
- 2 tbsp pumpkin seeds
- 2 tbsp lemon juice
- 1 clove garlic
- ½ tsp white miso paste
- 1 can chickpeas
- 1 tsp olive oil

Directions:
1. Place the chickpeas in the air fryer and cook at 200°C for 12 minutes
2. Cook the pasta according to packet instructions
3. Add the remaining ingredients to a food processor and blend
4. Add the pasta to a bowl and spoon over the pesto mix
5. Serve and top with roasted chickpeas

Ratatouille

Servings: 4
Cooking Time:xx
Ingredients:
- ½ small aubergine, cubed
- 1 courgette, cubed
- 1 tomato, cubed
- 1 pepper, cut into cubes
- ½ onion, diced
- 1 fresh cayenne pepper, sliced
- 1 tsp vinegar
- 5 sprigs basil, chopped
- 2 sprigs oregano, chopped
- 1 clove garlic, crushed
- Salt and pepper
- 1 tbsp olive oil
- 1 tbsp white wine

Directions:
1. Preheat air fryer to 200°C
2. Place all ingredients in a bowl and mix
3. Pour into a baking dish
4. Add dish to the air fryer and cook for 8 minutes, stir then cook for another 10 minutes

Roast Vegetables

Servings: 4
Cooking Time:xx
Ingredients:
- 100g diced courgette
- 100g diced squash
- 100g diced mushrooms
- 100g diced cauliflower
- 100g diced asparagus
- 100g diced pepper
- 2 tsp oil
- ½ tsp salt
- ¼ tsp pepper
- ¼ tsp seasoning

Directions:
1. Preheat air fryer to 180°C
2. Mix all ingredients together
3. Add to air fryer and cook for 10 minutes stirring halfway

Onion Dumplings

Servings: 2
Cooking Time:xx
Ingredients:
- 14 frozen dumplings (pierogies)
- 1 onion
- 1 tbsp olive oil
- 1 tsp sugar

Directions:
1. Take a large saucepan and fill with water, bringing to the boil
2. Cook the dumplings for 5 minutes, remove and drain
3. Slice the onion into long pieces
4. Oil the air fryer basket and preheat to 220°C
5. Cook the onion for 12 minutes, stirring often. After 5 minutes, add the sugar and combine
6. Remove the onions and place to one side
7. Add the dumplings to the air fryer and cook for 4 minutes
8. Turn the temperature up to 270°C and cook for another 3 minutes
9. Mix the dumplings with the onions before serving

Courgette Burgers

Servings: 4
Cooking Time:xx

Ingredients:
- 1 courgette
- 1 small can of chickpeas, drained
- 3 spring onions
- Pinch of dried garlic
- Salt and pepper
- 3 tbsp coriander
- 1 tsp chilli powder
- 1 tsp mixed spice
- 1 tsp cumin

Directions:
1. Grate the courgette and drain the excess water
2. Thinly slice the spring onions and add to the bowl with the chickpeas, courgette and seasoning
3. Bind the ingredients and form into patties
4. Place in the air fryer and cook for 12 minutes at 200°C

Rainbow Vegetables

Servings: 4
Cooking Time:xx

Ingredients:
- 1 red pepper, cut into slices
- 1 squash sliced
- 1 courgette sliced
- 1 tbsp olive oil
- 150g sliced mushrooms
- 1 onion sliced
- Salt and pepper to taste

Directions:
1. Preheat air fryer to 180°C
2. Place all ingredients in a bowl and mix well
3. Place in the air fryer and cook for about 20 minutes turning halfway

Jackfruit Taquitos

Servings: 2
Cooking Time:xx
Ingredients:
- 1 large Jackfruit
- 250g red beans
- 100g pico de gallo sauce
- 50ml water
- 2 tbsp water
- 4 wheat tortillas
- Olive oil spray

Directions:
1. Place the jackfruit, red beans, sauce and water in a saucepan
2. Bring to the boil and simmer for 25 minutes
3. Preheat the air fryer to 185°C
4. Mash the jackfruit mixture, add ¼ cup of the mix to each tortilla and roll up tightly
5. Spray with olive oil and place in the air fryer
6. Cook for 8 minutes

Potato Gratin

Servings: 4
Cooking Time:xx
Ingredients:
- 2 large potatoes
- 2 beaten eggs
- 100ml coconut cream
- 1 tbsp plain flour
- 50g grated cheddar

Directions:
1. Slice the potatoes into thin slices, place in the air fryer and cook for 10 minutes at 180°C
2. Mix eggs, coconut cream and flour together
3. Line four ramekins with the potato slices
4. Cover with the cream mixture, sprinkle with cheese and cook for 10 minutes at 200°C

Air-fried Artichoke Hearts

Servings: 7
Cooking Time:xx
Ingredients:
- 14 artichoke hearts
- 200g flour
- ¼ tsp baking powder
- Salt
- 6 tbsp water
- 6 tbsp breadcrumbs
- ¼ tsp basil
- ¼ tsp oregano
- ¼ tsp garlic powder
- ¼ tsp paprika

Directions:
1. Mix the baking powder, salt, flour and water in a bowl
2. In another bowl combine the breadcrumbs and seasonings
3. Dip the artichoke in the batter then coat in breadcrumbs
4. Place in the air fryer and cook at 180°C for 8 minutes

Spring Ratatouille

Servings:2
Cooking Time:15 Minutes
Ingredients:
- 1 tbsp olive oil
- 4 Roma tomatoes, sliced
- 2 cloves garlic, minced
- 1 courgette, cut into chunks
- 1 red pepper and 1 yellow pepper, cut into chunks
- 2 tbsp mixed herbs
- 1 tbsp vinegar

Directions:
1. Preheat the air fryer to 190 °C / 370 °F and line the air fryer with parchment paper or grease it with olive oil.
2. Place all of the ingredients into a large mixing bowl and mix until fully combined.
3. Transfer the vegetables into the lined air fryer basket, close the lid, and cook for 15 minutes until the vegetables have softened.

Shakshuka

Servings: 2
Cooking Time:xx

Ingredients:

- 2 eggs
- BASE
- 100 g/3½ oz. thinly sliced (bell) peppers
- 1 red onion, halved and thinly sliced
- 2 medium tomatoes, chopped
- 2 teaspoons olive oil
- ¼ teaspoon salt
- ¼ teaspoon freshly ground black pepper
- ½ teaspoon chilli/hot red pepper flakes
- SAUCE
- 100 g/3½ oz. passata/strained tomatoes
- 1 tablespoon tomato purée/paste
- 1 teaspoon balsamic vinegar
- ½ teaspoon runny honey
- ½ teaspoon ground cumin
- ½ teaspoon paprika
- ¼ teaspoon salt
- ⅛ teaspoon freshly ground black pepper

Directions:

1. Preheat the air-fryer to 180°C/350°F.
2. Combine the base ingredients together in a baking dish that fits inside your air-fryer. Add the dish to the preheated air-fryer and air-fry for 10 minutes, stirring halfway through cooking.
3. Meanwhile, combine the sauce ingredients in a bowl. Pour this into the baking dish when the 10 minutes are up. Stir, then make a couple of wells in the sauce for the eggs. Crack the eggs into the wells, then cook for a further 5 minutes or until the eggs are just cooked and yolks still runny. Remove from the air-fryer and serve.

Macaroni & Cheese Quiche

Servings: 4
Cooking Time:xx

Ingredients:
- 8 tbsp macaroni pasta
- 1 block of short crust pastry
- 2 tbsp Greek yogurt
- 2 eggs
- 150ml milk
- 1 tsp garlic puree
- 400g grated cheese

Directions:
1. Rub the inside of 4 ramekins with flour
2. Line the ramekins with the pastry
3. Mix the yogurt, garlic and macaroni. Add to the ramekins until ¾ full
4. Mix the egg and milk together and pour over the macaroni. Sprinkle with cheese
5. Heat the air fryer to 180°C and cook for 20 minutes until golden brown.

Gnocchi Caprese

Servings: 2
Cooking Time:xx

Ingredients:
- 1 packet of gnocchi
- 150g cherry tomatoes, cut into halves
- 2 tbsp olive oil
- 2 tbsp balsamic vinegar
- 3 pressed cloves of garlic
- 200g basil, chopped
- 200g mini mozzarella balls
- 150g grated Parmesan
- Salt and pepper for seasoning

Directions:
1. Preheat the air fryer to 220°C
2. Take a large bowl and add the cherry tomatoes, gnocchi, oil, balsamic vinegar, garlic and seasoning, making sure that everything is well coated
3. Transfer to the air fryer basket
4. Cook for 10 minutes, shaking the basket every few minutes
5. Once cooked, transfer everything to a large mixing bowl and add the Parmesan cheese, coating well
6. Then, add the mozzarella and basil and toss once more

Lentil Burgers

Servings: 4
Cooking Time:xx
Ingredients:
- 100g black buluga lentils
- 1 carrot, grated
- 1 diced onion
- 100g white cabbage
- 300g oats
- 1 tbsp garlic puree
- 1 tsp cumin
- Salt and pepper

Directions:
1. Blend the oats until they resemble flour
2. Put the lentils in a pan with water and cook for 45 minutes
3. Steam your vegetables for 5 minutes
4. Add all the ingredients into a bowl and mix well to combine
5. Form into burgers place in the air fryer and cook at 180°C for 30 minutes

Saganaki

Servings: 2
Cooking Time:xx
Ingredients:
- 200 g/7 oz. kefalotyri or manouri cheese, sliced into wedges 1 cm/½ in. thick
- 2 tablespoons plain/all-purpose flour
- olive oil, for drizzling

Directions:
1. Preheat the air-fryer to 200°C/400°F.
2. Dip each wedge of cheese in the flour, then tap off any excess. Drizzle olive oil onto both sides of the cheese slices
3. Add the cheese to the preheated air-fryer and air-fry for 3 minutes. Remove from the air-fryer and serve.

Mini Quiche

Servings: 2
Cooking Time:xx

Ingredients:

- 100g raw cashews
- 3 tbsp milk
- ½ tsp hot sauce
- 1 tsp white miso paste
- 1 tsp mustard
- 300g tofu
- 100g bacon pieces
- 1 chopped red pepper
- 1 chopped onion
- 6 tbsp yeast
- ½ tsp onion powder
- ½ tsp paprika
- ½ tsp cumin
- ½ tsp chilli powder
- ½ tsp black pepper
- ⅛ tsp turmeric
- ½ tsp canola oil
- 50g curly kale

Directions:

1. Heat the oil in a pan, add the bacon pepper, onion and curly kale and cook for about 3 minutes
2. Place all the other ingredients into a blender and blend until smooth
3. Add to a bowl with the bacon, pepper, onion and curly kale and mix well
4. Fill silicone muffin cups with the mix
5. Place in the air fryer and cook at 165°C for 15 minutes

Veggie Bakes

Servings: 2
Cooking Time:xx

Ingredients:

- Any type of leftover vegetable bake you have
- 30g flour

Directions:

1. Preheat the air fryer to 180°C
2. Mix the flour with the leftover vegetable bake
3. Shape into balls and place in the air fryer
4. Cook for 10 minutes

Goat's Cheese Tartlets

Servings: 2
Cooking Time:xx
Ingredients:
- 1 readymade sheet of puff pastry, 35 x 23 cm/14 x 9 in. (gluten-free if you wish)
- 4 tablespoons pesto (jarred or see page 80)
- 4 roasted baby (bell) peppers (see page 120)
- 4 tablespoons soft goat's cheese
- 2 teaspoons milk (plant-based if you wish)

Directions:
1. Cut the pastry sheet in half along the long edge, to make two smaller rectangles. Fold in the edges of each pastry rectangle to form a crust. Using a fork, prick a few holes in the base of the pastry. Brush half the pesto onto each rectangle, top with the peppers and goat's cheese. Brush the pastry crust with milk.
2. Preheat the air-fryer to 180°C/350°F.
3. Place one tartlet on an air-fryer liner or a piece of pierced parchment paper in the preheated air-fryer and air-fry for 6 minutes (you'll need to cook them one at a time). Repeat with the second tartlet.

Vegan Meatballs

Servings:4
Cooking Time:15 Minutes
Ingredients:
- 2 tbsp olive oil
- 2 tbsp soy sauce
- 1 onion, finely sliced
- 1 large carrot, peeled and grated
- 1 x 400 g / 14 oz can chickpeas, drained and rinsed
- 50 g / 1.8 oz plain flour
- 50 g / 1.8 oz rolled oats
- 2 tbsp roasted cashews, chopped
- 1 tsp garlic powder
- ½ tsp cumin

Directions:
1. Preheat the air fryer to 175 °C / 350 °F and line the air fryer with parchment paper or grease it with olive oil.
2. In a large mixing bowl, combine the olive oil and soy sauce. Add the onion slices and grated carrot and toss to coat in the sauce.
3. Place the vegetables in the air fryer and cook for 5 minutes until slightly soft.
4. Meanwhile, place the chickpeas, plain flour, rolled oats, and roasted cashews in a blender, and mix until well combined.
5. Remove the mixture from the blender and stir in the garlic powder and cumin. Add the onions and carrots to the bowl and mix well.
6. Scoop the mixture into small meatballs and place them into the air fryer. Increase the temperature on the machine up to 190 °C / 370 °F and cook the meatballs for 10-12 minutes until golden and crispy.

Spinach And Feta Croissants

Servings:4
Cooking Time:10 Minutes
Ingredients:
- 4 pre-made croissants
- 100 g / 7 oz feta cheese, crumbled
- 1 tsp dried chives
- 1 tsp garlic powder
- 50 g / 3.5 oz fresh spinach, chopped

Directions:
1. Preheat the air fryer to 180 °C / 350 °F. Remove the mesh basket from the air fryer machine and line with parchment paper.
2. Cut the croissants in half and lay each half out on the lined mesh basket.
3. In a bowl, combine the crumbled feta cheese, dried chives, garlic powder, and chopped spinach until they form a consistent mixture.
4. Spoon some of the mixture one half of the four croissants and cover with the second half of the croissants to seal in the filling.
5. Carefully slide the croissants in the mesh basket into the air fryer machine, close the lid, and cook for 10 minutes until the pastry is crispy and the feta cheese has melted.

Paneer Tikka

Servings: 2
Cooking Time:xx
Ingredients:
- 200ml yogurt
- 1 tsp ginger garlic paste
- 1 tsp red chilli powder
- 1 tsp garam masala
- 1 tsp turmeric powder
- 1 tbsp dried fenugreek leaves
- The juice of 1 lemon
- 2 tbsp chopped coriander
- 1 tbsp olive oil
- 250g paneer cheese, cut into cubes
- 1 green pepper, chopped
- 1 red pepper, chopped
- 1 yellow pepper, chopped
- 1 chopped onion

Directions:
1. Take a mixing bowl and add the yogurt, garlic paste, red chilli powder, garam masala, turmeric powder, lemon juice, fenugreek and chopped coriander, combining well
2. Place the marinade to one side
3. Add the cubed cheese to the marinade and toss to coat well
4. Leave to marinade for 2 hours
5. Take 8 skewers and alternate the cheese with the peppers and onions
6. Drizzle a little oil over the top
7. Arrange in the air fryer and cook at 220°C for 3 minutes
8. Turn and cook for another 3 minutes

Beef & Lamb And Pork Recipes

Sweet And Sticky Ribs

Servings: 2
Cooking Time: 1 Hour 15 Minutes

Ingredients:
- 500 g / 17.6 oz pork ribs
- 2 cloves garlic, minced
- 2 tbsp soy sauce
- 2 tsp honey
- 1 tbsp cayenne pepper
- 1 tsp olive oil
- 2 tbsp BBQ sauce
- 1 tsp salt
- 1 tsp black pepper

Directions:
1. Place the pork ribs on a clean surface and cut them into smaller chunks if necessary.
2. In a small mixing bowl, combine the minced garlic, soy sauce, 1 tsp honey, cayenne pepper, olive oil, BBQ sauce, salt, and pepper. Rub the pork ribs into the sauce and spice the mixture until fully coated.
3. Place the coated ribs in the fridge for 1 hour. Meanwhile, preheat the air fryer to 180 °C / 350 °F and line the bottom of the basket with parchment paper.
4. After one hour, transfer the pork ribs into the prepared air fryer basket. Close the lid and cook for 15 minutes, using tongs to turn them halfway through.
5. Once cooked, remove the ribs from the air fryer and use a brush to top each rib with the remaining 1 tsp honey.
6. Return the ribs to the air fryer for a further 2-3 minutes to heat the honey glaze before serving.

Beef Kebobs

Servings: 4
Cooking Time: xx

Ingredients:
- 500g cubed beef
- 25g low fat sour cream
- 2 tbsp soy sauce
- 8 x 6 inch skewers
- 1 bell pepper
- Half an onion

Directions:
1. Mix the sour cream and soy sauce in a bowl, add the cubed beef and marinate for at least 30 minutes
2. Cut the pepper and onion into 1 inch pieces, soak the skewers in water for 10 minutes
3. Thread beef, bell peppers and onion onto skewers
4. Cook in the air fryer at 200°C for 10 minutes turning halfway

Mongolian Beef

Servings: 4
Cooking Time:xx
Ingredients:
- 500g steak
- 25g cornstarch
- 2 tsp vegetable oil
- ½ tsp ginger
- 1 tbsp garlic minced
- 75g soy sauce
- 75g water
- 100g brown sugar

Directions:
1. Slice the steak and coat in corn starch
2. Place in the air fryer and cook at 200°C for 10 minutes turning halfway
3. Place remaining ingredients in a sauce pan and gently warm
4. When cooked place the steak in a bowl and pour the sauce over

Steak And Mushrooms

Servings: 4
Cooking Time:xx
Ingredients:
- 500g cubed sirloin steak
- 300g button mushrooms
- 3 tbsp Worcestershire sauce
- 1 tbsp olive oil
- 1 tsp parsley flakes
- 1 tsp paprika
- 1 tsp crushed chilli flakes

Directions:
1. Combine all ingredients in a bowl, cover and chill for at least 4 hours
2. Preheat air fryer to 200°C
3. Drain and discard the marinade from the steak
4. Place the steak and mushrooms in the air fryer and cook for 5 minutes
5. Toss and cook for a further 5 minutes

Tahini Beef Bites

Servings: 2
Cooking Time:xx
Ingredients:
- 500g sirloin steak, cut into cubes
- 2 tbsp Za'atar seasoning
- 1 tsp olive oil
- 25g Tahini
- 25g warm water
- 1 tbsp lemon juice
- 1 clove of garlic
- Salt to taste

Directions:
1. Preheat the air fryer to 250°C
2. Take a bowl and combine the oil with the steak, salt, and Za'atar seasoning
3. Place in the air fryer and cook for 10 minutes, turning halfway through
4. Take a bowl and combine the water, garlic, lemon juice, salt, and tahini, or use a food processor if you have one
5. Pour the sauce over the bites and serve

Pork Schnitzel

Servings: 2
Cooking Time:xx
Ingredients:
- 3 pork steaks, cut into cubes
- Salt and pepper
- 175g flour
- 2 eggs
- 175g breadcrumbs

Directions:
1. Sprinkle the pork with salt and pepper
2. Coat in the flour then dip in the egg
3. Coat the pork in breadcrumbs
4. Place in the air fryer and cook at 175°C for 20 minutes turning halfway
5. Serve with red cabbage

Buttermilk Pork Chops

Servings: 4
Cooking Time:xx
Ingredients:
- 4 pork chops
- 3 tbsp buttermilk
- 75g flour
- Cooking oil spray
- 1 packet of pork rub
- Salt and pepper to taste

Directions:
1. Rub the chops with the pork rub
2. Place the pork chops in a bowl and drizzle with buttermilk
3. Coat the chops with flour
4. Place in the air fryer and cook at 190°C for 15 minutes turning halfway

Hamburgers With Feta

Servings: 4
Cooking Time:xx
Ingredients:
- 400g minced beef
- 250g crumbled feta
- 25g chopped green olives
- ½ tsp garlic powder
- ½ cup chopped onion
- 2 tbsp Worcestershire sauce
- ½ tsp steak seasoning
- Salt to taste

Directions:
1. Mix all the ingredients in a bowl
2. Divide the mix into four and shape into patties
3. Place in the air fryer and cook at 200°C for about 15 minutes

Carne Asada Chips

Servings: 2
Cooking Time:xx

Ingredients:

- 500g sirloin steak
- 1 bag of frozen French fries
- 350g grated cheese
- 2 tbsp sour cream
- 2 tbsp guacamole
- 2 tbsp steak seasoning
- Salt and pepper to taste

Directions:

1. Preheat your oven to 260°C
2. Season the steak with the seasoning and a little salt and pepper
3. Place in the air fryer and cook for 4 minutes, before turning over and cooking for another 4 minutes
4. Remove and allow to rest
5. Add the French fries to the fryer and cook for 5 minutes, shaking regularly
6. Add the cheese
7. Cut the steak into pieces and add on top of the cheese
8. Cook for another 30 seconds, until the cheese is melted
9. Season

Steak Fajitas

Servings: 4
Cooking Time:xx

Ingredients:

- 500g sliced steak
- 25g pineapple juice
- 2 tbsp lime juice
- 1 tbsp olive oil
- 1 tbsp soy sauce
- 1 tbsp minced garlic
- ½ tbsp chilli powder
- 1/2 tsp paprika
- 1 tsp cumin
- 1 pepper
- 1 onion
- Salt and pepper to taste

Directions:

1. Mix pineapple juice, lime juice, olive oil, soy sauce, garlic, cumin chilli powder and paprika. Pour over the steak and marinate for 4 hours
2. Line the air fryer with foil, add the peppers and onions, season with salt and pepper
3. Cook at 200°C for 10 minutes, add the steak and cook for another 7 minutes
4. Serve with tortillas
5. Set your fryer to 170°C and cook the sandwich for 4 minutes
6. Turn the sandwich over and cook for another 3 minutes
7. Turn the sandwich out and serve whilst hot
8. Repeat with the other remaining sandwich

Lamb Burgers

Servings: 4
Cooking Time:xx

Ingredients:
- 600g minced lamb
- 2 tsp garlic puree
- 1 tsp harissa paste
- 2 tbsp Moroccan spice
- Salt and pepper

Directions:
1. Place all the ingredients in a bowl and mix well
2. Form into patties
3. Place in the air fryer and cook at 180°C for 18 minutes

Steak Dinner

Servings: 5
Cooking Time:xx

Ingredients:
- 400g sirloin steak, cut into cubes
- 300g red potatoes, cubed
- 1 pepper
- 1 tsp dried parsley
- ½ tsp pepper
- 2 tsp olive oil
- 1 sliced onion
- 300g chopped mushrooms
- 2 tsp garlic salt
- 2 tsp salt
- 5 tsp butter

Directions:
1. Preheat the air fryer to 200°C
2. Take 5 pieces of foil, layer meat onion, potatoes, mushrooms and pepper in each one
3. Add 1 tsp of butter to each one
4. Mix seasonings and sprinkle over the top
5. Fold the foil and cook for 25-30 minutes

Roast Beef

Servings: 2
Cooking Time:xx
Ingredients:
- 400g beef fillet
- 1 tbsp olive oil
- 1 tsp salt
- 1 tsp rosemary

Directions:
1. Preheat the air fryer to 180°C
2. Mix salt, rosemary and oil on a plate
3. Coat the beef with the mix
4. Place the beef in the air fryer and cook for 45 minutes turning halfway

Salt And Pepper Belly Pork

Servings: 4
Cooking Time:xx
Ingredients:
- 500g belly pork
- 1 tsp pepper
- ½ tsp salt

Directions:
1. Cut the pork into bite size pieces and season with salt and pepper
2. Heat the air fryer to 200°C
3. Place in the air fryer and cook for 15 minutes until crisp

German Rouladen

Servings: 2
Cooking Time:xx
Ingredients:
- 2 tbsp oil
- 2 cups sliced onion
- 4 tbsp sour cream
- 1 tbsp tomato paste
- 1 tsp chopped parsley
- 400g steak
- ¼ cup dijon mustard
- 4 bacon strips

Directions:
1. Add salt and pepper to the onions and mix
2. Cook the onions in the air fryer at 200°C for 5-6 minutes
3. Put half the onions in a bowl and mix with sour cream, 2 tsp parsley and tomato paste
4. Spread the mustard on to the steak then add the bacon and onion
5. Roll the steak up tightly and cook in the air fryer for 8-10 minutes

Italian Meatballs

Servings: 12
Cooking Time:xx

Ingredients:
- 2 tbsp olive oil
- 2 tbsp minced shallot
- 3 cloves garlic minced
- 100g panko crumbs
- 35g chopped parsley
- 1 tbsp chopped rosemary
- 60ml milk
- 400g minced pork
- 250g turkey sausage
- 1 egg beaten
- 1 tbsp dijon mustard
- 1 tbsp finely chopped thyme

Directions:
1. Preheat air fryer to 200°C
2. Heat oil in a pan and cook the garlic and shallot over a medium heat for 1-2 minutes
3. Mix the panko and milk in a bowl and allow to stand for 5 minutes
4. Add all the ingredients to the panko mix and combine well
5. Shape into 1 ½ inch meatballs and cook for 12 minutes

Honey & Mustard Meatballs

Servings: 4
Cooking Time:xx

Ingredients:
- 500g minced pork
- 1 red onion
- 1 tsp mustard
- 2 tsp honey
- 1 tsp garlic puree
- 1 tsp pork seasoning
- Salt and pepper

Directions:
1. Thinly slice the onion
2. Place all the ingredients in a bowl and mix until well combined
3. Form into meatballs, place in the air fryer and cook at 180°C for 10 minutes

Pork Taquitos

Servings: 5
Cooking Time:xx
Ingredients:
- 400g shredded pork
- 500g grated mozzarella
- 10 flour tortillas
- The juice of 1 lime
- Cooking spray

Directions:
1. Preheat air fryer to 190°C
2. Sprinkle lime juice on the pork and mix
3. Microwave tortilla for about 10 seconds to soften
4. Add a little pork and cheese to a tortilla
5. Roll then tortilla up, and place in the air fryer
6. Cook for about 7 minutes until golden, turn halfway through cooking

Meatballs In Tomato Sauce

Servings: 4
Cooking Time:xx
Ingredients:
- 1 small onion
- 300g minced pork
- 1 tbsp chopped parsley
- 1 tbsp thyme
- 1 egg
- 3 tbsp bread crumbs
- Salt and pepper to taste

Directions:
1. Place all ingredients into a bowl and mix well
2. Shape mixture into 12 meatballs
3. Heat the air fryer to 200°C
4. Place the meatballs into the air fryer and cook for about 7 minutes
5. Tip the meatballs into an oven dish add the tomato sauce and cook for about 5 minutes in the air fryer until warmed through

Pulled Pork, Bacon, And Cheese Sliders

Servings:2
Cooking Time:30 Minutes
Ingredients:
- 2 x 50 g / 3.5 oz pork steaks
- 1 tsp salt
- 1 tsp black pepper
- 4 slices bacon strips, chopped into small pieces
- 1 tbsp soy sauce
- 1 tbsp BBQ sauce
- 100 g / 7 oz cheddar cheese, grated
- 2 bread buns

Directions:
1. Preheat the air fryer to 200 °C / 400 °F and line the bottom of the basket with parchment paper.
2. Place the pork steaks on a clean surface and season with salt and black pepper. Move the pork steak in the prepared air fryer basket and cook for 15 minutes.
3. Remove the steak from the air fryer and shred using two forks. Mix with the chopped bacon in a heatproof bowl and place the bowl in the air fryer. Cook for 10 minutes.
4. Remove the bowl from the air fryer and stir in the soy sauce and BBQ sauce. Return the bowl to the air fryer basket and continue cooking for a further 5 minutes.
5. Meanwhile, spread the cheese across one half of the bread buns. Top with the cooked pulled pork and an extra squirt of BBQ sauce.

Breaded Pork Chops

Servings: 6
Cooking Time:xx
Ingredients:
- 6 boneless pork chops
- 1 beaten egg
- 100g panko crumbs
- 75g crushed cornflakes
- 2 tbsp parmesan
- 1 ¼ tsp paprika
- ½ tsp garlic powder
- ½ tsp onion powder
- ¼ tsp chilli powder
- Salt and pepper to taste

Directions:
1. Heat the air fryer to 200°C
2. Season the pork chops with salt
3. Mix the panko, cornflakes, salt, parmesan, garlic powder, onion powder, paprika, chilli powder and pepper in a bowl
4. Beat the egg in another bowl
5. Dip the pork in the egg and then coat with panko mix
6. Place in the air fryer and cook for about 12 minutes turning halfway

Vegetable & Beef Frittata

Servings: 2
Cooking Time:xx

Ingredients:
- 250g ground beef
- 4 shredded hash browns
- 8 eggs
- Half a diced onion
- 1 courgette, diced
- 250g grated cheese
- Salt and pepper for seasoning

Directions:
1. Break the ground beef up and place in the air fryer
2. Add the onion and combine well
3. Cook at 260°C for 3 minutes
4. Stir the mixture and cook foremother 2 minutes
5. Remove and clean the tray
6. Add the courgette to the air fryer and spray with a little cooking oil
7. Cook for 3 minutes
8. Add to the meat mixture and combine
9. Take a mixing bowl and combine the cheese, has browns, and eggs
10. Add the meat and courgette to the bowl and season with salt and pepper
11. Take a 6" round baking tray and add the mixture
12. Cook for 8 minutes before cutting lines in the top and cooking for another 8 minutes
13. Cut into slices before serving

Chinese Chilli Beef

Servings: 2
Cooking Time:xx

Ingredients:
- 4 tbsp light soy sauce
- 1 tsp honey
- 3 tbsp tomato ketchup
- 1 tsp Chinese 5 spice
- 1 tbsp oil
- 6 tbsp sweet chilli sauce
- 1 tbsp lemon juice
- 400g frying steak
- 2 tbsp cornflour

Directions:
1. Slice the steak into strips, put into a bowl and cover with cornflour and 5 spice
2. Add to the air fryer and cook for 6 minutes at 200°C
3. Whilst the beef is cooking mix together the remaining ingredients
4. Add to the air fryer and cook for another 3 minutes

Poultry Recipes

Air Fryer Chicken Thigh Schnitzel

Servings: 4
Cooking Time: xx

Ingredients:
- 300g boneless chicken thighs
- 160g seasoned breadcrumbs
- 1 tsp salt
- ½ tsp ground black pepper
- 30g flour
- 1 egg
- Cooking spray

Directions:
1. Lay the chicken on a sheet of parchment paper and add another on top
2. Use a mallet or a rolling pin to flatten it down
3. Take a bowl and add the breadcrumbs with the salt and pepper
4. Place the flour into another bowl
5. Dip the chicken into the flour, then the egg, and then the breadcrumbs
6. Preheat air fryer to 190°C
7. Place the chicken into the air fryer and spray with cooking oil
8. Cook for 6 minutes

Air Fryer Bbq Chicken

Servings: 4
Cooking Time: xx

Ingredients:
- 1 whole chicken
- 2 tbsp avocado oil
- 1 tbsp kosher salt
- 1 tsp ground pepper
- 1 tsp garlic powder
- 1 tsp paprika
- ½ tsp dried basil
- ½ tsp dried oregano
- ½ tsp dried thyme

Directions:
1. Mix the seasonings together and spread over chicken
2. Place the chicken in the air fryer breast side down
3. Cook at 182C for 50 minutes and then breast side up for 10 minutes
4. Carve and serve

Chicken & Potatoes

Servings: 4
Cooking Time:xx

Ingredients:

- 2 tbsp olive oil
- 2 potatoes, cut into 2" pieces
- 2 chicken breasts, cut into pieces of around 1" size
- 4 crushed garlic cloves
- 2 tsp smoked paprika
- 1 tsp thyme
- 1/2 tsp red chilli flakes
- Salt and pepper to taste

Directions:

1. Preheat your air fryer to 260°C
2. Take a large bowl and combine the potatoes with half of the garlic, half the paprika, half the chilli flakes, salt, pepper and half the oil
3. Place into the air fryer and cook for 5 minutes, before turning over and cooking for another 5 minutes
4. Take a bowl and add the chicken with the rest of the seasonings and oil, until totally coated
5. Add the chicken to the potatoes mixture, moving the potatoes to the side
6. Cook for 10 minutes, turning the chicken halfway through

Pepper & Lemon Chicken Wings

Servings: 2
Cooking Time:xx

Ingredients:

- 1kg chicken wings
- 1/4 tsp cayenne pepper
- 2 tsp lemon pepper seasoning
- 3 tbsp butter
- 1 tsp honey
- An extra 1 tsp lemon pepper seasoning for the sauce

Directions:

1. Preheat the air fryer to 260°C
2. Place the lemon pepper seasoning and cayenne in a bowl and combine
3. Coat the chicken in the seasoning
4. Place the chicken in the air fryer and cook for 20 minutes, turning over halfway
5. Turn the temperature up to 300°C and cook for another 6 minutes
6. Meanwhile, melt the butter and combine with the honey and the rest of the seasoning
7. Remove the wings from the air fryer and pour the sauce over the top

Turkey Cutlets In Mushroom Sauce

Servings: 2
Cooking Time:xx
Ingredients:
- 2 turkey cutlets
- 1 tbsp butter
- 1 can of cream of mushroom sauce
- 160ml milk
- Salt and pepper for seasoning

Directions:
1. Preheat the air fryer to 220°C
2. Brush the turkey cults with the butter and seasoning
3. Place in the air fryer and cook for 11 minutes
4. Add the mushroom soup and milk to a pan and cook over the stone for around 10 minutes, stirring every so often
5. Top the turkey cutlets with the sauce

Chicken And Wheat Stir Fry

Servings: 4
Cooking Time:xx
Ingredients:
- 1 onion
- 1 clove of garlic
- 200g skinless boneless chicken breast halves
- 3 whole tomatoes
- 400ml water
- 1 chicken stock cube
- 1 tbsp curry powder
- 130g wheat berries
- 1 tbsp vegetable oil

Directions:
1. Thinly slice the onion and garlic
2. Chop the chicken and tomatoes into cubes
3. Take a large saucepan and add the water, chicken stock, curry powder and wheat berries, combining well
4. Pour the oil into the air fryer bowl and heat for 5 minutes at 200°C
5. Add the remaining ingredients and pour the contents into the air fryer
6. Cook for 15 minutes

Cheddar & Bbq Stuffed Chicken

Servings: 2
Cooking Time:xx

Ingredients:

- 3 strips of bacon
- 100g cheddar cheese
- 3 tbsp barbecue sauce
- 300g skinless and boneless chicken breasts
- salt and ground pepper to taste

Directions:

1. Preheat the air fryer to 190°C
2. Cook one of the back strips for 2 minutes, before cutting into small pieces
3. Increase the temperature of the air fryer to 200°C
4. Mix together the cooked bacon, cheddar cheese and 1 tbsp barbecue sauce
5. Take the chicken and make a pouch by cutting a 1 inch gap into the top
6. Stuff the pouch with the bacon and cheese mixture and then wrap around the chicken breast
7. Coat the chicken with the rest of the BBQ sauce
8. Cook for 10 minutes in the air fryer, before turning and cooking for an additional 10 minutes

Crispy Cornish Hen

Servings: 4
Cooking Time:xx

Ingredients:

- 2 Cornish hens, weighing around 500g each
- 2 tbsp olive oil
- 1 tsp garlic powder
- 1 tsp paprika
- 1.5 tsp Italian seasoning
- 1 tbsp lemon juice
- Salt and pepper to taste

Directions:

1. Preheat your air fryer to 260°C
2. Combine all the ingredients into a bowl (except for the hens) until smooth
3. Brush the hens with the mixture, coating evenly
4. Place in the air fryer basket, with the breast side facing down
5. Cook for 35 minutes
6. Turn over and cook for another 10 minutes
7. Ensure the hens are white in the middle before serving

Turkey And Mushroom Burgers

Servings: 2
Cooking Time:xx

Ingredients:
- 180g mushrooms
- 500g minced turkey
- 1 tbsp of your favourite chicken seasoning, e.g. Maggi
- 1 tsp onion powder
- 1 tsp garlic powder
- Salt and pepper to taste

Directions:
1. Place the mushrooms in a food processor and puree
2. Add all the seasonings and mix well
3. Remove from the food processor and transfer to a mixing bowl
4. Add the minced turkey and combine again
5. Shape the mix into 5 burger patties
6. Spray with cooking spray and place in the air fryer
7. Cook at 160°C for 10 minutes, until cooked.

Chicken Parmesan With Marinara Sauce

Servings: 4
Cooking Time:xx

Ingredients:
- 400g chicken breasts, sliced in half
- 250g panko breadcrumbs
- 140g grated parmesan cheese
- 140g grated mozzarella cheese
- 3 egg whites
- 200g marinara sauce
- 2 tsp Italian seasoning
- Salt and pepper to taste
- Cooking spray

Directions:
1. Preheat the air fryer to 200°C
2. Lay the chicken slices on the work surface and pound with a mallet or a rolling pin to flatten
3. Take a mixing bowl and add the panko breadcrumbs, cheese and the seasoning, combining well
4. Add the egg whites into a separate bowl
5. Dip the chicken into the egg whites and then the breadcrumbs
6. Cook for 7 minutes in the air fryer

Smoky Chicken Breast

Servings: 2
Cooking Time:xx
Ingredients:
- 2 halved chicken breasts
- 2 tsp olive oil
- 1 tsp ground thyme
- 2 tsp paprika
- 1tsp cumin
- 0.5 tsp cayenne pepper
- 0.5 tsp onion powder
- Salt and pepper to taste

Directions:
1. In a medium bowl, combine the spices together
2. Pour the spice mixture onto a plate
3. Take each chicken breast and coat in the spices, pressing down to ensure an even distribution
4. Place the chicken to one side for 5 minutes
5. Preheat your air fryer to 180°C
6. Arrange the chicken inside the fryer and cook for 10 minutes
7. Turn the chicken over and cook for another 10 minutes
8. Remove from the fryer and allow to sit for 5 minutes before serving

Spicy Chicken Wing Drummettes

Servings: 4
Cooking Time:xx
Ingredients:
- 10 large chicken drumettes
- Cooking spray
- 100ml rice vinegar
- 3 tbsp honey
- 2 tbsp unsalted chicken stock
- 1 tbsp lower sodium soy sauce
- 1 tbsp toasted sesame oil
- ⅜ tsp crushed red pepper
- 1 garlic clove, finely chopped
- 2 tbsp chopped, unsalted, roasted peanuts
- 1 tbsp chopped fresh chives

Directions:
1. Coat the chicken in cooking spray and place inside the air fryer
2. Cook at 200°C for 30 minutes
3. Take a mixing bowl and combine the vinegar, honey, stock, soy sauce, oil, crushed red pepper and garlic
4. Cook to a simmer, until a syrup consistency is achieved
5. Coat the chicken in this mixture and sprinkle with peanuts and chives

Nashville Chicken

Servings: 4
Cooking Time:xx

Ingredients:
- 400g boneless chicken breast tenders
- 2 tsp salt
- 2 tsp coarsely ground black pepper
- 2 tbsp hot sauce
- 2 tbsp pickle juice
- 500g all purpose flour
- 3 large eggs
- 300ml buttermilk
- 2 tbsp olive oil
- 6 tbsp cayenne pepper
- 3 tbsp dark brown sugar
- 1 tsp chilli powder
- 1 tsp garlic powder
- 1 tsp paprika
- Salt and pepper to taste

Directions:
1. Take a large mixing bowl and add the chicken, hot sauce, pickle juice, salt and pepper and combine
2. Place in the refrigerator for 3 hours
3. Transfer the flour to a bowl
4. Take another bowl and add the eggs, buttermilk and 1 tbsp of the hot sauce, combining well
5. Press each piece of chicken into the flour and coat well
6. Place the chicken into the buttermilk mixture and then back into the flour
7. Allow to sit or 10 minutes
8. Preheat the air fryer to 193C
9. Whisk together the spices, brown sugar and olive oil to make the sauce and pour over the chicken tenders
10. Serve whilst still warm

Chicken Tikka Masala

Servings: 4
Cooking Time:xx
Ingredients:
- 100g tikka masala curry pasta
- 200g low fat yogurt
- 600g skinless chicken breasts
- 1 tbsp vegetable oil
- 1 onion, chopped
- 400g can of the whole, peeled tomatoes
- 20ml water
- 1 tbsp sugar
- 2 tbsp lemon juice
- 1 small bunch of chopped coriander leaves

Directions:
1. Take a bowl and combine the tikka masala curry paste with half the yogurt
2. Cut the chicken into strips
3. Preheat the air fryer to 200°C
4. Add the yogurt mixture and coat the chicken until fully covered
5. Place into the refrigerator for 2 hours
6. Place the oil and onion in the air fryer and cook for 10 minutes
7. Add the marinated chicken, tomatoes, water and the rest of the yogurt and combine
8. Add the sugar and lemon juice and combine again
9. Cook for 15 minutes

Chicken Milanese

Servings: 4
Cooking Time:xx
Ingredients:
- 130 g/1¾ cups dried breadcrumbs (gluten-free if you wish, see page 9)
- 50 g/⅔ cup grated Parmesan
- 1 teaspoon dried basil
- ½ teaspoon dried thyme
- ¼ teaspoon freshly ground black pepper
- 1 egg, beaten
- 4 tablespoons plain/all-purpose flour (gluten-free if you wish)
- 4 boneless chicken breasts

Directions:
1. Combine the breadcrumbs, cheese, herbs and pepper in a bowl. In a second bowl beat the egg, and in the third bowl have the plain/all-purpose flour. Dip each chicken breast first into the flour, then the egg, then the seasoned breadcrumbs.
2. Preheat the air-fryer to 180°C/350°F.
3. Add the breaded chicken breasts to the preheated air-fryer and air-fry for 12 minutes. Check the internal temperature of the chicken has reached at least 74°C/165°F using a meat thermometer – if not, cook for another few minutes.

Quick Chicken Nuggets

Servings: 4
Cooking Time:xx

Ingredients:

- 500g chicken tenders
- 25g ranch salad dressing mixture
- 2 tbsp plain flour
- 100g breadcrumbs
- 1 egg, beaten
- Olive oil spray

Directions:

1. Take a large mixing bowl and arrange the chicken inside
2. Sprinkle the seasoning over the top and ensure the chicken is evenly coated
3. Place the chicken to one side for around 10 minutes
4. Add the flour into a resealable bag
5. Crack the egg into a small mixing bowl and whisk
6. Pour the breadcrumbs onto a medium sized plate
7. Transfer the chicken into the resealable bag and coat with the flour, giving it a good shake
8. Remove the chicken and dip into the egg, and then rolling it into the breadcrumbs, coating evenly
9. Repeat with all pieces of the chicken
10. Heat your air fryer to 200°C
11. Arrange the chicken inside the fryer and add a little olive oil spray to avoid sticking
12. Cook for 4 minutes, before turning over and cooking for another 4 minutes
13. Remove and serve whilst hot

Chicken Kiev

Servings: 4
Cooking Time:xx

Ingredients:

- 4 boneless chicken breasts
- 4 tablespoons plain/all-purpose flour (gluten-free if you wish)
- 1 egg, beaten
- 130 g/2 cups dried breadcrumbs (gluten-free if you wish, see page 9)
- GARLIC BUTTER
- 60 g/4 tablespoons salted butter, softened
- 1 large garlic clove, finely chopped

Directions:

1. Mash together the butter and garlic. Form into a sausage shape, then slice into 4 equal discs. Place in the freezer until frozen.
2. Make a deep horizontal slit across each chicken breast, taking care not to cut through to the other side. Stuff the cavity with a disc of frozen garlic butter. Place the flour in a shallow bowl, the egg in another and the breadcrumbs in a third. Coat each chicken breast first in flour, then egg, then breadcrumbs.
3. Preheat the air-fryer to 180°C/350°F.
4. Add the chicken Kievs to the preheated air-fryer and air-fry for 12 minutes until cooked through. This is hard to gauge as the butter inside the breast is not an indicator of doneness, so test the meat in the centre with a meat thermometer – it should be at least 75°C/167°F; if not, cook for another few minutes.

Air Fried Maple Chicken Thighs

Servings: 4
Cooking Time:xx
Ingredients:
- 200ml buttermilk
- ½ tbsp maple syrup
- 1 egg
- 1 tsp granulated garlic salt
- 4 chicken thighs with the bone in
- 140g all purpose flour
- 65g tapioca flour
- 1 tsp sweet paprika
- 1 tsp onion powder
- ¼ tsp ground black pepper
- ¼ tsp cayenne pepper
- ½ tsp granulated garlic
- ½ tsp honey powder

Directions:
1. Take a bowl and combine the buttermilk, maple syrup, egg and garlic powder
2. Transfer to a bag and add chicken thighs, shaking to combine well
3. Set aside for 1 hour
4. Take a shallow bowl and add the flour, tapioca flour, salt, sweet paprika, smoked paprika, pepper, cayenne pepper and honey powder, combining well
5. Preheat the air fryer to 190ºC
6. Drag the chicken through flour mixture and place the chicken skin side down in the air fryer Cook for 12 minutes, until white in the middle

Cornflake Chicken Nuggets

Servings: 4
Cooking Time:xx
Ingredients:
- 100 g/4 cups cornflakes (gluten-free if you wish)
- 70 g/½ cup plus ½ tablespoon plain/all-purpose flour (gluten-free if you wish)
- 2 eggs, beaten
- ½ teaspoon salt
- ¼ teaspoon freshly ground black pepper
- 600 g/1 lb. 5 oz. mini chicken fillets

Directions:
1. Grind the cornflakes in a food processor to a crumb-like texture. Place the flour in one bowl and the beaten eggs in a second bowl; season both bowls with the salt and pepper. Coat each chicken fillet in flour, tapping off any excess. Next dip each flour-coated chicken fillet into the egg, then the cornflakes until fully coated.
2. Preheat the air-fryer to 180ºC/350ºF.
3. Add the chicken fillets to the preheated air-fryer (you may need to add the fillets in two batches, depending on the size of your air-fryer) and air-fry for 10 minutes, turning halfway through cooking. Check the internal temperature of the nuggets has reached at least 74ºC/165ºF using a meat thermometer – if not, cook for another few minutes and then serve.
4. VARIATION: SIMPLE CHICKEN NUGGETS
5. For a simpler version, replace the crushed cornflakes with 90 g/1¼ cups dried breadcrumbs (see page 9). Prepare and air-fry in the same way.

Buffalo Wings

Servings: 4
Cooking Time:xx

Ingredients:

- 500g chicken wings
- 1 tbsp olive oil
- 5 tbsp cayenne pepper sauce
- 75g butter
- 2 tbsp vinegar
- 1 tsp garlic powder
- ¼ tsp cayenne pepper

Directions:

1. Preheat the air fryer to 182C
2. Take a large mixing bowl and add the chicken wings
3. Drizzle oil over the wings, coating evenly
4. Cook for 25 minutes and then flip the wings and cook for 5 more minutes
5. In a saucepan over a medium heat, mix the hot pepper sauce, butter, vinegar, garlic powder and cayenne pepper, combining well
6. Pour the sauce over the wings and flip to coat, before serving

Chicken Jalfrezi

Servings: 4
Cooking Time:xx

Ingredients:

- 500g chicken breasts
- 1 tbsp water
- 4 tbsp tomato sauce
- 1 chopped onion
- 1 chopped bell pepper
- 2 tsp love oil
- 1 tsp turmeric
- 1 tsp cayenne pepper
- 2 tsp garam masala
- Salt and pepper to taste

Directions:

1. Take a large mixing bowl and add the chicken, onions, pepper, salt, garam masala, turmeric, oil and cayenne pepper, combining well
2. Place the chicken mix in the air fryer and cook at 180°C for 15 minutes
3. Take a microwave-safe bowl and add the tomato sauce, water salt, garam masala and cayenne, combining well
4. Cook in the microwave for 1 minute, stir then cook for a further minute
5. Remove the chicken from the air fryer and pour the sauce over the top.
6. Serve whilst still warm

Pizza Chicken Nuggets

Servings: 2
Cooking Time:xx

Ingredients:

- 60 g/¾ cup dried breadcrumbs (see page 9)
- 20 g/¼ cup grated Parmesan
- ½ teaspoon dried oregano
- ¼ teaspoon freshly ground black pepper
- 150 g/⅔ cup Mediterranean sauce (see page 102) or 150 g/5½ oz. jarred tomato pasta sauce (keep any leftover sauce for serving)
- 400 g/14 oz. chicken fillets

Directions:

1. Preheat the air-fryer to 180°C/350°F.
2. Combine the breadcrumbs, Parmesan, oregano and pepper in a bowl. Have the Mediterranean or pasta sauce in a separate bowl.
3. Dip each chicken fillet in the tomato sauce first, then roll in the breadcrumb mix until coated fully.
4. Add the breaded fillets to the preheated air-fryer and air-fry for 10 minutes. Check the internal temperature of the chicken has reached at least 74°C/165°F using a meat thermometer – if not, cook for another few minutes.
5. Serve with some additional sauce that has been warmed through.

Satay Chicken Skewers

Servings: 4
Cooking Time:xx

Ingredients:

- 3 chicken breasts, chopped into 3 x 3-cm/1¼ x 1¼-in. cubes
- MARINADE
- 200 ml/¾ cup canned coconut milk (including the thick part from the can)
- 1 plump garlic clove, finely chopped
- 2 teaspoons freshly grated ginger
- 2 tablespoons soy sauce
- 1 heaped tablespoon peanut butter
- 1 tablespoon maple syrup
- 1 tablespoon mild curry powder
- 1 tablespoon fish sauce

Directions:

1. Mix the marinade ingredients thoroughly in a bowl, then toss in the chopped chicken and stir to coat thoroughly. Leave in the fridge to marinate for at least 4 hours.
2. Preheat the air-fryer to 190°C/375°F.
3. Thread the chicken onto 8 metal skewers. Add to the preheated air-fryer (you may need to cook these in two batches, depending on the size of your air-fryer). Air-fry for 10 minutes. Check the internal temperature of the chicken has reached at least 74°C/165°F using a meat thermometer – if not, cook for another few minutes and then serve.

Fish & Seafood Recipes

Air Fried Scallops

Servings: 2
Cooking Time: xx
Ingredients:
- 6 scallops
- 1 tbsp olive oil
- Salt and pepper to taste

Directions:
1. Brush the filets with olive oil
2. Sprinkle with salt and pepper
3. Place in the air fryer and cook at 200°C for 2 mins
4. Turn the scallops over and cook for another 2 minutes

Copycat Fish Fingers

Servings: 2
Cooking Time: xx
Ingredients:
- 2 slices wholemeal bread, grated into breadcrumbs
- 50g plain flour
- 1 beaten egg
- 1 white fish fillet
- The juice of 1 small lemon
- 1 tsp parsley
- 1 tsp thyme
- 1 tsp mixed herbs
- Salt and pepper to taste

Directions:
1. Preheat the air fryer to 180°C
2. Add salt pepper and parsley to the breadcrumbs and combine well
3. Place the egg in another bowl
4. Place the flour in a separate bowl
5. Place the fish into a food processor and add the lemon juice, salt, pepper thyme and mixed herbs
6. Blitz to create a crumb-like consistency
7. Roll your fish in the flour, then the egg and then the breadcrumbs
8. Cook at 180°C for 8 minutes

Fish In Foil

Servings: 2
Cooking Time: xx
Ingredients:
- 1 tablespoon avocado oil or olive oil, plus extra for greasing
- 1 tablespoon soy sauce (or tamari)
- 1½ teaspoons freshly grated garlic
- 1½ teaspoons freshly grated ginger
- 1 small red chilli/chile, finely chopped
- 2 skinless, boneless white fish fillets (about 350 g/12 oz. total weight)

Directions:
1. Mix the oil, soy sauce, garlic, ginger and chilli/chile together. Brush a little oil onto two pieces of foil, then lay the fish in the centre of the foil. Spoon the topping mixture over the fish. Wrap the foil around the fish to make a parcel, with a gap above the fish but shallow enough to fit in your air-fryer basket.
2. Preheat the air-fryer to 180°C/350°F.
3. Add the foil parcels to the preheated air-fryer and air-fry for 7–10 minutes, depending on the thickness of your fillets. The fish should just flake when a fork is inserted. Serve immediately.

Cajun Shrimp Boil

Servings: 6
Cooking Time: xx
Ingredients:
- 300g cooked shrimp
- 14 slices of smoked sausage
- 5 par boiled potatoes, cut into halves
- 4 mini corn on the cobs, quartered
- 1 diced onion
- 3 tbsp old bay seasoning
- Olive oil spray

Directions:
1. Combine all the ingredients in a bowl and mix well
2. Line the air fryer with foil
3. Place half the mix into the air fryer and cook at 200°C for about 6 minutes, mix the ingredients and cook for a further 6 minutes.
4. Repeat for the second batch

Parmesan-coated Fish Fingers

Servings: 2
Cooking Time:xx
Ingredients:
- 350 g/12 oz. cod loins
- 1 tablespoon grated Parmesan
- 40 g/½ cup dried breadcrumbs (gluten-free if you wish, see page 9)
- 1 egg, beaten
- 2 tablespoons plain/all-purpose flour (gluten free if you wish)

Directions:
1. Slice the cod into 6 equal fish fingers/sticks.
2. Mix the Parmesan together with the breadcrumbs. Lay out three bowls: one with flour, one with beaten egg and the other with the Parmesan breadcrumbs. Dip each fish finger/stick first into the flour, then the egg and then the breadcrumbs until fully coated.
3. Preheat the air-fryer to 180°C/350°F.
4. Add the fish to the preheated air-fryer and air-fry for 6 minutes. Check the internal temperature of the fish has reached at least 75°C/167°F using a meat thermometer – if not, cook for another few minutes. Serve immediately.

Mahi Fish Tacos

Servings: 4
Cooking Time:xx
Ingredients:
- 400g fresh mahi
- 8 small corn tortillas
- 2 tsp cajun seasoning
- 5 tbsp sour cream
- 2 tbsp mayonnaise
- 2 tbsp scotch bonnet pepper sauce (use 1 tbsp if you don't like your food too spicy)
- 1 tbsp sriracha sauce
- 2 tbsp lime juice
- Salt and pepper to taste
- 1 tbsp vegetable oil

Directions:
1. Clean the mahi. Cut into half inch slices and season with salt
2. Mix quarter parts cayenne pepper and black pepper with cajun seasoning. Sprinkle onto fish
3. Brush pepper sauce on both sides of the fish
4. Set the air fryer to 180°C and cook for about 10 minutes or until golden brown
5. Whilst the fish cooks make the chipotle lime cream. Mix the mayo, sour cream, lime juice sriracha and cayenne pepper
6. Assemble tacos and enjoy

Extra Crispy Popcorn Shrimp

Servings: 2
Cooking Time:xx
Ingredients:
- 300g Frozen popcorn shrimp
- 1 tsp cayenne pepper
- Salt and pepper for seasoning

Directions:
1. Preheat the air fryer to 220°C
2. Place the shrimp inside the air fryer and cook for 6 minutes, giving them a shake at the halfway point
3. Remove and season with salt and pepper, and the cayenne to your liking

Fish In Parchment Paper

Servings: 2
Cooking Time:xx
Ingredients:
- 250g cod fillets
- 1 chopped carrot
- 1 chopped fennel
- 1 tbsp oil
- 1 thinly sliced red pepper
- ½ tsp tarragon
- 1 tbsp lemon juice
- 1 tbsp salt
- ½ tsp ground pepper

Directions:
1. In a bowl, mix the tarragon and ½ tsp salt add the vegetables and mix well
2. Cut two large squares of parchment paper
3. Spray the cod with oil and cover both sides with salt and pepper
4. Place the cod in the parchment paper and add the vegetables
5. Fold over the paper to hold the fish and vegetables
6. Place in the air fryer and cook at 170°C for 15 minutes

Thai Fish Cakes

Servings: 4
Cooking Time:xx

Ingredients:
- 200g pre-mashed potatoes
- 2 fillets of white fish, flaked and mashed
- 1 onion
- 1 tsp butter
- 1 tsp milk
- 1 lime zest and rind
- 3 tsp chilli
- 1 tsp Worcester sauce
- 1 tsp coriander
- 1 tsp mixed spice
- 1 tsp mixed herbs
- 50g breadcrumbs
- Salt and pepper to taste

Directions:
1. Cover the white fish in milk
2. in a mixing bowl place the fish and add the seasoning and mashed potatoes
3. Add the butter and remaining milk
4. Use your hands to create patties and place in the refrigerator for 3 hours
5. Preheat your air fryer to 200°C
6. Cook for 15 minutes

Shrimp With Yum Yum Sauce

Servings: 4
Cooking Time:xx

Ingredients:
- 400g peeled jumbo shrimp
- 1 tbsp soy sauce
- 1 tbsp garlic paste
- 1 tbsp ginger paste
- 4 tbsp mayo
- 2 tbsp ketchup
- 1 tbsp sugar
- 1 tsp paprika
- 1 tsp garlic powder

Directions:
1. Mix soy sauce, garlic paste and ginger paste in a bowl. Add the shrimp, allow to marinate for 15 minutes
2. In another bowl mix ketchup, mayo, sugar, paprika and the garlic powder to make the yum yum sauce.
3. Set the air fryer to 200°C, place shrimp in the basket and cook for 8-10 minutes

Salt & Pepper Calamari

Servings: 2
Cooking Time:xx
Ingredients:
- 500g squid rings
- 500g panko breadcrumbs
- 250g plain flour
- 2 tbsp pepper
- 2 tbsp salt
- 200ml buttermilk
- 1 egg

Directions:
1. Take a medium bowl and combine the buttermilk and egg, stirring well
2. Take another bowl and combine the salt, pepper, flour, and panko breadcrumbs, combining again
3. Dip the quid into the buttermilk first and then the breadcrumbs, coating evenly
4. Place in the air fryer basket
5. Cook at 150°C for 12 minutes, until golden

Fish Taco Cauliflower Rice Bowls

Servings: 2
Cooking Time:xx
Ingredients:
- 400g fish of your choice, cut into strips
- 1 tsp chilli powder
- ½ tsp paprika
- 1 sliced avocado
- 25g pickled red onions
- 25g reduced fat sour cream
- ½ tsp cumin
- Salt and pepper to taste
- 300g cauliflower rice
- 1 tbsp lime juice
- 25g fresh coriander
- 1 tbsp sriracha

Directions:
1. Sprinkle both sides of the fish with chilli powder, cumin, paprika, salt and pepper
2. Heat the air fryer to 200°C, cook the fish for about 12 minutes
3. cook the cauliflower rice according to instructions, mix in lime juice and coriander once cooked
4. Divide the cauliflower rice between two bowls, add the sliced avocado, fish and pickled red onions.
5. Mix the sour cream with the sriracha and drizzle over the top

Store-cupboard Fishcakes

Servings: 3
Cooking Time:xx
Ingredients:
- 400 g/14 oz. cooked potato – either mashed potato or the insides of jacket potatoes (see page 124)
- 2 x 150–200-g/5½–7-oz. cans fish, such as tuna or salmon, drained
- 2 eggs
- ¾ teaspoon salt
- 1 teaspoon dried parsley
- ½ teaspoon freshly ground black pepper
- 1 tablespoon olive oil
- caper dressing (see page 79), to serve

Directions:
1. Mix the cooked potato, fish, eggs, salt, parsley and pepper together in a bowl, then divide into 6 equal portions and form into fishcakes. Drizzle the olive oil over both sides of each fishcake.
2. Preheat the air-fryer to 180°C/350°F.
3. Add the fishcakes to the preheated air-fryer and air-fry for 15 minutes, turning halfway through cooking. Serve with salad and tartare sauce or Caper Dressing.

Gluten Free Honey And Garlic Shrimp

Servings: 2
Cooking Time:xx
Ingredients:
- 500g fresh shrimp
- 5 tbsp honey
- 2 tbsp gluten free soy sauce
- 2 tbsp tomato ketchup
- 250g frozen stir fry vegetables
- 1 crushed garlic clove
- 1 tsp fresh ginger
- 2 tbsp cornstarch

Directions:
1. Simmer the honey, soy sauce, garlic, tomato ketchup and ginger in a saucepan
2. Add the cornstarch and whisk until sauce thickens
3. Coat the shrimp with the sauce
4. Line the air fryer with foil and add the shrimp and vegetables
5. Cook at 180°C for 10 minutes

Chilli Lime Tilapia

Servings: 3
Cooking Time:xx
Ingredients:
- 500g Tilapia fillets
- 25g panko crumbs
- 200g flour
- Salt and pepper to taste
- 2 eggs
- 1 tbsp chilli powder
- The juice of 1 lime

Directions:
1. Mix panko, salt and pepper and chilli powder together
2. Whisk the egg in a separate bowl
3. Spray the air fryer with cooking spray
4. Dip the tilapia in the flour, then in the egg and cover in the panko mix
5. Place fish in the air fryer, spray with cooking spray and cook for 7-8 minutes at 190°C
6. Turn the fish over and cook for a further 7-8 minutes until golden brown.
7. Squeeze lime juice over the top and serve

Garlic Tilapia

Servings: 2
Cooking Time:xx
Ingredients:
- 2 tilapia fillets
- 2 tsp chopped fresh chives
- 2 tsp chopped fresh parsley
- 2 tsp olive oil
- 1 tsp minced garlic
- Salt and pepper for seasoning

Directions:
1. Preheat the air fryer to 220°C
2. Take a small bowl and combine the olive oil with the chives, garlic, parsley and a little salt and pepper
3. Brush the mixture over the fish fillets
4. Place the fish into the air fryer and cook for 10 minutes, until flaky

Honey Sriracha Salmon

Servings: 2
Cooking Time:xx
Ingredients:
- 25g sriracha
- 25g honey
- 500g salmon fillets
- 1 tbsp soy sauce

Directions:
1. Mix the honey, soy sauce and sriracha, keep half the mix to one side for dipping
2. Place the salmon in the sauce skin side up and marinade for 30 minutes
3. Spray air fryer basket with cooking spray
4. Heat the air fryer to 200°C
5. Place salmon in the air fryer skin side down and cook for 12 minutes

Ranch Style Fish Fillets

Servings: 4
Cooking Time:xx
Ingredients:
- 200g bread crumbs
- 30g ranch-style dressing mix
- 2 tbsp oil
- 2 beaten eggs
- 4 fish fillets of your choice
- Lemon wedges to garnish

Directions:
1. Preheat air fryer to 180°C
2. Mix the bread crumbs and ranch dressing mix together, add in the oil until the mix becomes crumbly
3. Dip the fish into the, then cover in the breadcrumb mix
4. Place in the air fryer and cook for 12-13 minutes

Cajun Prawn Skewers

Servings: 2
Cooking Time:xx
Ingredients:
- 350 g/12 oz. king prawns/jumbo shrimp
- MARINADE
- 1 teaspoon smoked paprika
- 1 teaspoon unrefined sugar
- 1 teaspoon salt
- ½ teaspoon onion powder
- ½ teaspoon mustard powder
- ¼ teaspoon dried oregano
- ¼ teaspoon dried thyme
- 1 teaspoon white wine vinegar
- 2 teaspoons olive oil

Directions:
1. Mix all the marinade ingredients together in a bowl. Mix the prawns/shrimp into the marinade and cover. Place in the fridge to marinate for at least an hour.
2. Preheat the air-fryer to 180°C/350°F.
3. Thread 4–5 prawns/shrimp on to each skewer (you should have enough for 4–5 skewers). Add the skewers to the preheated air-fryer and air-fry for 2 minutes, then turn the skewers and cook for a further 2 minutes. Check the internal temperature of the prawns/shrimp has reached at least 50°C/125°F using a meat thermometer – if not, cook for another few minutes. Serve immediately.

Air Fryer Mussels

Servings: 2
Cooking Time:xx
Ingredients:
- 400g mussels
- 1 tbsp butter
- 200ml water
- 1 tsp basil
- 2 tsp minced garlic
- 1 tsp chives
- 1 tsp parsley

Directions:
1. Preheat air fryer to 200°C
2. Clean the mussels, soak for 30 minutes, and remove the beard
3. Add all ingredients to an air fryer-safe pan
4. Cook for 3 minutes
5. Check to see if the mussels have opened, if not cook for a further 2 minutes. Once all mussels are open, they are ready to eat.

Crunchy Fish

Servings: 4
Cooking Time:xx

Ingredients:

- 200g dry breadcrumbs
- 4 tbsp olive oil
- 4 fillets of white fish
- 1 beaten egg
- 1 sliced lemon

Directions:

1. Heat the fryer to 180°C
2. In a medium mixing bowl, combine the olive oil and the breadcrumbs
3. Take the fish and first dip it into the egg and then the breadcrumbs, making sure they are evenly coated well
4. Arrange the fish into the basket
5. Cook for 12 minutes
6. Remove and serve with lemon slices

Cod Nuggets

Servings: 4
Cooking Time:xx

Ingredients:

- 400g cod fillets, cut into 8 chunks
- 35g flour
- 1 tbsp vegetable oil
- 200g cornflakes or cracker crumbs
- Egg wash - 1 tbsp egg and 1 tbsp water
- Salt and pepper to taste

Directions:

1. Crush the crackers or cornflakes to make crumbs, mix in the vegetable oil
2. Season the cod with salt and pepper and cover in flour, dip into the egg-wash then cover in crumbs
3. Set the air fryer to 180°C
4. Place the cod nuggets in the air fryer basket and cook for 15 minutes, until golden brown.

Thai-style Tuna Fishcakes

Servings: 2
Cooking Time:xx

Ingredients:

- 200 g/7 oz. cooked potato
- 145 g/5 oz. canned tuna, drained
- 60 g/1 cup canned sweetcorn/corn kernels (drained weight)
- ½ teaspoon soy sauce
- ½ teaspoon fish sauce
- ½ teaspoon Thai 7 spice
- freshly squeezed juice of ½ a lime
- 1 teaspoon freshly grated garlic
- 1 teaspoon freshly grated ginger
- avocado or olive oil, for brushing
- LIME-ALMOND SATAY SAUCE
- 20 ml/4 teaspoons fresh lime juice
- 2 heaped tablespoons almond butter
- 1 teaspoon soy sauce
- ½ teaspoon freshly grated ginger
- ½ teaspoon freshly grated garlic
- ½ teaspoon avocado or olive oil
- ½ teaspoon maple syrup

Directions:

1. Combine all the fishcake ingredients in a food processor and blend together. Divide the mixture into 6 equal portions and mould into fishcakes. Brush a little oil over the top surface of the fishcakes.
2. Preheat the air-fryer to 180°C/350°F.
3. Place the fishcakes on an air-fryer liner or a piece of pierced parchment paper and add to the preheated air-fryer. Air-fry for 4 minutes, then turn over and brush the other side of each fishcake with oil and air-fry for a further 4 minutes.
4. To make the satay dipping sauce, mix all ingredients in a bowl with 1 tablespoon warm water. Serve alongside the fishcakes.

Side Dishes Recipes

Potato Wedges With Rosemary

Servings: 2
Cooking Time:xx

Ingredients:

- 2 potatoes, sliced into wedges
- 1 tbsp olive oil
- 2 tsp seasoned salt
- 2 tbsp chopped rosemary

Directions:

1. Preheat air fryer to 190°C
2. Drizzle potatoes with oil, mix in salt and rosemary
3. Place in the air fryer and cook for 20 minutes turning halfway

Cheesy Garlic Asparagus

Servings: 4
Cooking Time:xx

Ingredients:

- 1 tsp olive oil
- 500g asparagus
- 1 tsp garlic salt
- 1 tbsp grated parmesan cheese
- Salt and pepper for seasoning

Directions:

1. Preheat the air fryer to 270°C
2. Clean the asparagus and cut off the bottom 1"
3. Pat dry and place in the air fryer, covering with the oil
4. Sprinkle the parmesan and garlic salt on top, seasoning to your liking
5. Cook for between 7 and 10 minutes
6. Add a little extra parmesan over the top before serving

Aubergine Parmesan

Servings: 4
Cooking Time:xx

Ingredients:

- 100g Italian breadcrumbs
- 50g grated parmesan
- 1 tsp Italian seasoning
- 1 tsp salt
- ½ tsp dried basil
- ½ tsp onion powder
- ½ tsp black pepper
- 100g flour
- 2 eggs
- 1 aubergine, sliced into ½ inch rounds

Directions:

1. Mix breadcrumbs, parmesan, salt Italian seasoning, basil, onion powder and pepper in a bowl
2. Add the flour to another bowl, and beat the eggs in another
3. Dip the aubergine in the flour, then the eggs and then coat in the bread crumbs
4. Preheat the air fryer to 185°C
5. Place the aubergine in the air fryer and cook for 8-10 minutes
6. Turnover and cook for a further 4-6 minutes

Yorkshire Puddings

Servings: 2
Cooking Time:xx

Ingredients:

- 1 tablespoon olive oil
- 70 g/½ cup plus ½ tablespoon plain/all-purpose flour (gluten-free if you wish)
- 100 ml/7 tablespoons milk
- 2 eggs
- salt and freshly ground black pepper

Directions:

1. You will need 4 ramekins. Preheat the air-fryer to 200°C/400°F.
2. Using a pastry brush, oil the base and sides of each ramekin, dividing the oil equally between the ramekins. Place the greased ramekins in the preheated air-fryer and heat for 5 minutes.
3. Meanwhile, in a food processor or using a whisk, combine the flour, milk, eggs and seasoning until you have a batter that is frothy on top. Divide the batter equally between the preheated ramekins. Return the ramekins to the air-fryer and air-fry for 20 minutes without opening the drawer. Remove the Yorkshire puddings from the ramekins and serve immediately.

Orange Tofu

Servings: 4
Cooking Time:xx
Ingredients:
- 400g tofu, drained
- 1 tbsp tamari
- 1 tbsp corn starch
- ¼ tsp pepper flakes
- 1 tsp minced ginger
- 1 tsp fresh garlic
- 1 tsp orange zest
- 75ml orange juice
- 75ml water
- 2 tsp cornstarch
- 1 tbsp maple syrup

Directions:
1. Cut the tofu into cubes, place in a bowl add the tamari and mix well
2. Mix in 1 tbsp starch and allow to marinate for 30 minutes
3. Place the remaining ingredients into another bowl and mix well
4. Place the tofu in the air fryer and cook at 190°C for about 10 minutes
5. Add tofu to a pan with sauce mix and cook until sauce thickens

Super Easy Fries

Servings: 2
Cooking Time:xx
Ingredients:
- 500g potatoes cut into ½ inch sticks
- 1 tsp olive oil
- ¼ tsp salt
- ¼ tsp pepper

Directions:
1. Place the potatoes in a bowl cover with water and allow to soak for 30 minutes
2. Spread the butter onto one side of the bread slices
3. Pat dry with paper, drizzle with oil and toss to coat
4. Place in the air fryer and cook at 200°C for about 15 minutes, keep tossing through cooking time
5. Sprinkle with salt and pepper

Shishito Peppers

Servings: 2
Cooking Time:xx

Ingredients:
- 200g shishito peppers
- Salt and pepper to taste
- ½ tbsp avocado oil
- 75g grated cheese
- 2 limes

Directions:
1. Rinse the peppers
2. Place in a bowl and mix with oil, salt and pepper
3. Place in the air fryer and cook at 175°C for 10 minutes
4. Place on a serving plate and sprinkle with cheese

Potato Wedges

Servings: 4
Cooking Time:xx

Ingredients:
- 2 potatoes, cut into wedges
- 1 ½ tbsp olive oil
- ½ tsp paprika
- ⅛ tsp ground black pepper
- ½ tsp parsley flakes
- ½ tsp chilli powder
- ½ tsp sea salt

Directions:
1. Preheat the air fryer to 200°C
2. Add all ingredients to a bowl and combine well
3. Place the wedges into the air fryer and cook for 10 minutes
4. Turn and cook for a further 8 minutes until golden brown

Asparagus Spears

Servings: 2
Cooking Time:xx
Ingredients:
- 1 bunch of trimmed asparagus
- 1 teaspoon olive oil
- ¼ teaspoon salt
- ⅛ teaspoon freshly ground black pepper

Directions:
1. Preheat the air-fryer to 180°C/350°F.
2. Toss the asparagus spears in the oil and seasoning. Add these to the preheated air-fryer and air-fry for 8–12 minutes, turning once (cooking time depends on the thickness of the stalks, which should retain some bite).

Zingy Roasted Carrots

Servings: 4
Cooking Time:xx
Ingredients:
- 500g carrots
- 1 tsp olive oil
- 1 tsp cayenne pepper
- Salt and pepper for seasoning

Directions:
1. Peel the carrots and cut them into chunks, around 2" in size
2. Preheat your air fryer to 220°C
3. Add the carrots to a bowl with the olive oil and cayenne and toss to coat
4. Place in the fryer and cook for 15 minutes, giving them a stir halfway through
5. Season before serving

Butternut Squash Fries

Servings: 4
Cooking Time:xx
Ingredients:
- 400g butternut squash, cut into sticks
- 1 tbsp olive oil
- 2 tbsp bagel seasoning
- 1 tsp fresh chopped rosemary

Directions:
1. Preheat air fryer to 200°C
2. Drizzle butternut squash with olive oil mix to coat
3. Add to the air fryer, cook for about 22 minutes until golden brown, stirring every 4 minutes
4. Sprinkle with bagel seasoning to serve

Celery Root Fries

Servings: 2
Cooking Time:xx
Ingredients:
- ½ celeriac, cut into sticks
- 500ml water
- 1 tbsp lime juice
- 1 tbsp olive oil
- 75g mayo
- 1 tbsp mustard
- 1 tbsp powdered horseradish

Directions:
1. Put celeriac in a bowl, add water and lime juice, soak for 30 minutes
2. Preheat air fryer to 200
3. Mix together the mayo, horseradish powder and mustard, refrigerate
4. Drain the celeriac, drizzle with oil and season with salt and pepper
5. Place in the air fryer and cook for about 10 minutes turning halfway
6. Serve with the mayo mix as a dip

Orange Sesame Cauliflower

Servings: 4
Cooking Time:xx
Ingredients:
- 100ml water
- 30g cornstarch
- 50g flour
- 1/2 tsp salt
- ½ tsp pepper
- 2 tbsp tomato ketchup
- 2 tbsp brown sugar
- 1 sliced onion

Directions:
1. Mix together flour, cornstarch, water, salt and pepper until smooth
2. Coat the cauliflower and chill for 30 minutes
3. Place in the air fryer and cook for 22 minutes at 170°C
4. Meanwhile combine remaining ingredients in a saucepan, gently simmer until thickened.
5. Mix cauliflower with sauce and top with toasted sesame seeds to serve

Cauliflower With Hot Sauce And Blue Cheese Sauce

Servings:2
Cooking Time:15 Minutes
Ingredients:
- For the cauliflower:
- 1 cauliflower, broken into florets
- 4 tbsp hot sauce
- 2 tbsp olive oil
- 1 tsp garlic powder
- ½ tsp salt
- ½ tsp black pepper
- 1 tbsp plain flour
- 1 tbsp corn starch
- For the blue cheese sauce:
- 50 g / 1.8 oz blue cheese, crumbled
- 2 tbsp sour cream
- 2 tbsp mayonnaise
- ½ tsp salt
- ½ tsp black pepper

Directions:
1. Preheat the air fryer to 180 °C / 350 °F and line the bottom of the basket with parchment paper.
2. In a bowl, combine the hot sauce, olive oil, garlic powder, salt, and black pepper until it forms a consistent mixture. Add the cauliflower to the bowl and coat in the sauce.
3. Stir in the plain flour and corn starch until well combined.
4. Transfer the cauliflower to the lined basket in the air fryer, close the lid, and cook for 12-15 minutes until the cauliflower has softened and is golden in colour.
5. Meanwhile, make the blue cheese sauce by combining all of the ingredients. When the cauliflower is ready, remove it from the air fryer and serve with the blue cheese sauce on the side.

Honey Roasted Parsnips

Servings: 4
Cooking Time:xx
Ingredients:
- 350 g/12 oz. parsnips
- 1 tablespoon plain/all-purpose flour (gluten-free if you wish)
- 1½ tablespoons runny honey
- 2 tablespoons olive oil
- salt

Directions:
1. Top and tail the parsnips, then slice lengthways, about 2 cm/¾ in. wide. Place in a saucepan with water to cover and a good pinch of salt. Bring to the boil, then boil for 5 minutes.
2. Remove and drain well, allowing any excess water to evaporate. Dust the parsnips with flour. Mix together the honey and oil in a small bowl, then toss in the parsnips to coat well in the honey and oil.
3. Preheat the air-fryer to 180°C/350°F.
4. Add the parsnips to the preheated air-fryer and air-fry for 14–16 minutes, depending on how dark you like the outsides (the longer you cook them, the sweeter they get).

Whole Sweet Potatoes

Servings: 4 As A Side Or Snack
Cooking Time:xx

Ingredients:

- 4 medium sweet potatoes
- 1 tablespoon olive oil
- 1 teaspoon salt
- toppings of your choice

Directions:

1. Preheat the air-fryer to 200°C/400°F.
2. Wash and remove any imperfections from the skin of the sweet potatoes, then rub the potatoes with the olive oil and salt.
3. Add the sweet potatoes to the preheated air-fryer and air-fry for up to 40 minutes (the cooking time depends on the size of the potatoes). Remove as soon as they are soft when pierced. Slice open and serve with your choice of toppings.
4. VARIATION: WHOLE JACKET POTATOES
5. Regular baking potatoes can be air-fried in the same way, but will require a cooking time of 45–60 minutes, depending on their size.

Crispy Sweet & Spicy Cauliflower

Servings: 2
Cooking Time:xx

Ingredients:

- ½ a head of cauliflower
- 1 teaspoon sriracha sauce
- 1 teaspoon soy sauce (or tamari)
- ½ teaspoon maple syrup
- 2 teaspoons olive oil or avocado oil

Directions:

1. Preheat the air-fryer to 180°C/350°F.
2. Chop the cauliflower into florets with a head size of roughly 5 cm/1 in. Place the other ingredients in a bowl and mix together, then add the florets and toss to coat them.
3. Add the cauliflower to the preheated air-fryer and air-fry for 12 minutes, shaking the drawer a couple of times during cooking.

Crispy Broccoli

Servings: 2
Cooking Time:xx
Ingredients:
- 170 g/6 oz. broccoli florets
- 2 tablespoons olive oil
- ⅛ teaspoon garlic salt
- ⅛ teaspoon freshly ground black pepper
- 2 tablespoons freshly grated Parmesan or Pecorino

Directions:
1. Preheat the air-fryer to 200°C/400°F.
2. Toss the broccoli in the oil, season with the garlic salt and pepper, then toss over the grated cheese and combine well. Add the broccoli to the preheated air-fryer and air-fry for 5 minutes, giving the broccoli a stir halfway through to ensure even cooking.

Ricotta Stuffed Aubergine

Servings: 2
Cooking Time:xx
Ingredients:
- 1 aubergine
- 150g ricotta cheese
- 75g Parmesan cheese, plus an extra 75g for the breading
- 1 tsp garlic powder
- 3 tbsp parsley
- 1 egg, plus an extra 2 eggs for the breading
- 300g pork rind crumbs
- 2 tsp Italian seasoning

Directions:
1. Cut the aubergine into rounds, about 1/2" in thickness
2. Line a baking sheet with parchment and arrange the rounds on top, sprinkling with salt
3. Place another sheet of parchment on top and place something heavy on top to get rid of excess water
4. Leave for 30 minutes
5. Take a bowl and combine the egg, ricotta, 75g Parmesan and parsley, until smooth
6. Remove the parchment from the aubergine and wipe off the salt
7. Take a tablespoon of the ricotta mixture and place on top of each round of aubergine, spreading with a knife
8. Place in the freezer for a while to set
9. Take a bowl and add the two eggs, the pork rinds, parmesan and seasonings, and combine
10. Remove the aubergine from the freezer and coat each one in the mixture completely
11. Place back in the freezer for 45 minutes
12. Cook in the air fryer for 8 minutes at 250°C

Alternative Stuffed Potatoes

Servings: 4
Cooking Time:xx
Ingredients:
- 4 baking potatoes, peeled and halved
- 1 tbsp olive oil
- 150g grated cheese
- ½ onion, diced
- 2 slices bacon

Directions:
1. Preheat air fryer to 175°C
2. Brush the potatoes with oil and cook in the air fryer for 10 minutes
3. Coat again with oil and cook for a further 10 minutes
4. Cut the potatoes in half spoon the insides into a bowl and mix in the cheese
5. Place the bacon and onion in a pan and cook until browned, mix in with the potato
6. Stuff the skins with the mix and return to the air fryer, cook for about 6 minutes

Mediterranean Vegetables

Servings: 1–2
Cooking Time:xx
Ingredients:
- 1 courgette/zucchini, thickly sliced
- 1 (bell) pepper, deseeded and chopped into large chunks
- 1 red onion, sliced into wedges
- 12 cherry tomatoes
- 1 tablespoon olive oil
- ½ teaspoon salt
- ½ teaspoon freshly ground black pepper
- 2 rosemary twigs
- mozzarella, fresh pesto (see page 80) and basil leaves, to serve

Directions:
1. Preheat the air-fryer to 180°C/350°F.
2. Toss the prepared vegetables in the oil and seasoning. Add the vegetables and the rosemary to the preheated air-fryer and air-fry for 12–14 minutes, depending on how 'chargrilled' you like them.
3. Remove and serve topped with fresh mozzarella and pesto and scattered with basil leaves.

Crispy Cinnamon French Toast

Servings:2
Cooking Time:5 Minutes
Ingredients:
- 4 slices white bread
- 4 eggs
- 200 ml milk (cow's milk, cashew milk, soy milk, or oat milk)
- 2 tbsp granulated sugar
- 1 tsp brown sugar
- 1 tsp vanilla extract
- ½ tsp ground cinnamon

Directions:
1. Preheat your air fryer to 150 °C / 300 °F and line the bottom of the basket with parchment paper.
2. Cut each of the bread slices into 2 even rectangles and set them aside.
3. In a mixing bowl, whisk together the 4 eggs, milk, granulated sugar, brown sugar, vanilla extract, and ground cinnamon.
4. Soak the bread pieces in the egg mixture until they are fully covered and soaked in the mixture.
5. Place the coated bread slices in the lined air fryer, close the lid, and cook for 4-5 minutes until the bread is crispy and golden.
6. Serve the French toast slices with whatever toppings you desire.

Air Fryer Eggy Bread

Servings:2
Cooking Time:5-7 Minutes
Ingredients:
- 4 slices white bread
- 4 eggs, beaten
- 1 tsp black pepper
- 1 tsp dried chives

Directions:
1. Preheat your air fryer to 150 °C / 300 °F and line the bottom of the basket with parchment paper.
2. Whisk the eggs in a large mixing bowl and soak each slice of bread until fully coated.
3. Transfer the eggy bread to the preheated air fryer and cook for 5-7 minutes until the eggs are set and the bread is crispy.
4. Serve hot with a sprinkle of black pepper and chives on top.

Desserts Recipes

Strawberry Danish

Servings: 2
Cooking Time:xx
Ingredients:
- 1 tube crescent roll dough
- 200g cream cheese
- 25g strawberry jam
- 50g diced strawberries
- 225g powdered sugar
- 2-3 tbsp cream

Directions:
1. Roll out the dough
2. Spread the cream cheese over the dough, cover in jam
3. Sprinkle with strawberries
4. Roll the dough up from the short side and pinch to seal
5. Line the air fryer with parchment paper and spray with cooking spray
6. Place the dough in the air fryer and cook at 175°C for 20 minutes
7. Mix the cream with the powdered sugar and drizzle on top once cooked

Thai Fried Bananas

Servings: 8
Cooking Time:xx
Ingredients:
- 4 ripe bananas
- 2 tbsp flour
- 2 tbsp rice flour
- 2 tbsp cornflour
- 2 tbsp desiccated coconut
- Pinch salt
- ½ tsp baking powder
- ½ tsp cardamon powder

Directions:
1. Place all the dry ingredients in a bowl and mix well. Add a little water at a time and combine to form a batter
2. Cut the bananas in half and then half again length wise
3. Line the air fryer with parchment paper and spray with cooking spray
4. Dip each banana piece in the batter mix and place in the air fryer
5. Cook at 200°C for 10 -15 minutes turning halfway
6. Serve with ice cream

Cinnamon-maple Pineapple Kebabs

Servings: 2
Cooking Time:xx
Ingredients:
- 4 x pineapple strips, roughly 2 x 2 cm/¾ x ¾ in. by length of pineapple
- 1 teaspoon maple syrup
- ½ teaspoon vanilla extract
- ¼ teaspoon ground cinnamon
- Greek or plant-based yogurt and grated lime zest, to serve

Directions:
1. Line the air-fryer with an air-fryer liner or a piece of pierced parchment paper. Preheat the air-fryer to 180°C/350°F.
2. Stick small metal skewers through the pineapple lengthways. Mix the maple syrup and vanilla extract together, then drizzle over the pineapple and sprinkle over the cinnamon.
3. Add the skewers to the preheated lined air-fryer and air-fry for 15 minutes, turning once. If there is any maple-vanilla mixture left after the initial drizzle, then drizzle this over the pineapple during cooking too. Serve with yogurt and lime zest.

Cinnamon Biscuit Bites

Servings: 16
Cooking Time:xx
Ingredients:
- 200g flour
- 200g wholewheat flour
- 2 tbsp sugar
- 1 tsp baking powder
- ¼ tsp cinnamon
- ¼ tsp salt
- 4 tbsp butter
- 50ml milk
- Cooking spray
- 300g icing sugar
- 3 tbsp water

Directions:
1. Mix together flour, salt, sugar baking powder and cinnamon in a bowl
2. Add butter and mix until well combined
3. Add milk and form a dough, place dough on a floured surface and knead until smooth
4. Cut into 16 equal pieces and form each piece into a ball
5. Place in the air fryer and cook at 180°C for about 12 minutes
6. Mix together icing sugar and water and coat to serve

Brazilian Pineapple

Servings: 2
Cooking Time:xx
Ingredients:
- 1 small pineapple, cut into spears
- 100g brown sugar
- 2 tsp cinnamon
- 3 tbsp melted butter

Directions:
1. Mix the brown sugar and cinnamon together in a small bowl
2. Brush the pineapple with melted butter
3. Sprinkle with the sugar and cinnamon
4. Heat the air fryer to 200°C
5. Cook the pineapple for about 10 minutes

Chocolate Mug Cake

Servings: 1
Cooking Time:xx
Ingredients:
- 30g self raising flour
- 5 tbsp sugar
- 1 tbsp cocoa powder
- 3 tbsp milk
- 3 tsp coconut oil

Directions:
1. Mix all the ingredients together in a mug
2. Heat the air fryer to 200°C
3. Place the mug in the air fryer and cook for 10 minutes

Chocolate Cake

Servings: 2
Cooking Time:xx
Ingredients:
- 3 eggs
- 75ml sour cream
- 225g flour
- 150g sugar
- 2 tsp vanilla extract
- 25g cocoa powder
- 1 tsp baking powder
- ½ tsp baking soda

Directions:
1. Preheat the air fryer to 160°C
2. Mix all the ingredients together in a bowl
3. Pour into a greased baking tin
4. Place into the air fryer and cook for 25 minutes
5. Allow to cool and ice with chocolate frosting

White Chocolate And Raspberry Loaf

Servings:8
Cooking Time:1 Hour 10 Minutes
Ingredients:
- 400 g / 14 oz plain flour
- 2 tsp baking powder
- 1 tsp ground cinnamon
- ½ tsp salt
- 3 eggs, beaten
- 50 g / 3.5 oz granulated sugar
- 50 g / 3.5 oz brown sugar
- 100 g / 3.5 oz white chocolate chips
- 100 g / 3.5 oz fresh raspberries
- 1 tbsp cocoa powder
- 4 tbsp milk
- 1 tsp vanilla extract

Directions:
1. Preheat the air fryer to 150 °C / 300 °F and line a loaf tin with parchment paper.
2. Combine the plain flour, baking powder, ground cinnamon, and salt in a large mixing bowl.
3. Whisk eggs into the bowl, then stir in the granulated sugar and brown sugar. Mix well before folding in the white chocolate chips, fresh raspberries, cocoa powder, milk, and vanilla extract.
4. Stir the mixture until it is lump-free and transfer into a lined loaf tin. Place the loaf tin into the lined air fryer basket, close the lid, and cook for 30-40 minutes.
5. The cake should be golden and set by the end of the cooking process. Insert a knife into the centre of the cake. It should come out dry when the cake is fully cooked.
6. Remove the cake from the air fryer, still in the loaf tin. Set aside to cool on a drying rack for 20-30 minutes before cutting into slices and serving.

Peach Pies(1)

Servings: 8
Cooking Time:xx
Ingredients:
- 2 peaches, peeled and chopped
- 1 tbsp lemon juice
- 3 tbsp sugar
- 1 tsp vanilla extract
- ¼ tsp salt
- 1 tsp cornstarch
- 1 pack of shortcrust pastry

Directions:
1. Stir together peaches, lemon juice, sugar, vanilla and salt allow to stand for 15 minutes
2. Drain the peaches keeping 1 tbsp of the juice
3. Mix the liquid with the cornstarch and mix into the peaches
4. Cut out 8 4 inch circles from the pastry. Add 1 tbsp of peach mix to each piece of pastry
5. Fold the dough over to create half moons, crimp the edges with a fork to seal. Spray with cooking spray
6. Place in the air fryer and cook at 180°C for 12-14 minutes

Grilled Ginger & Coconut Pineapple Rings

Servings: 4
Cooking Time:xx
Ingredients:
- 1 medium pineapple
- coconut oil, melted
- 1½ teaspoons coconut sugar
- ½ teaspoon ground ginger
- coconut or vanilla yogurt, to serve

Directions:
1. Preheat the air-fryer to 180°C/350°F.
2. Peel and core the pineapple, then slice into 4 thick rings.
3. Mix together the melted coconut oil with the sugar and ginger in a small bowl. Using a pastry brush, paint this mixture all over the pineapple rings, including the sides of the rings.
4. Add the rings to the preheated air-fryer and air-fry for 20 minutes. Check after 18 minutes as pineapple sizes vary and your rings may be perfectly cooked already. You'll know they are ready when they're golden in colour and a fork can easily be inserted with very little resistance
5. Serve warm with a generous spoonful of yogurt.

Peanut Butter & Chocolate Baked Oats

Servings: 9
Cooking Time: xx

Ingredients:

- 150 g/1 heaped cup rolled oats/quick-cooking oats
- 50 g/⅓ cup dark chocolate chips or buttons
- 300 ml/1¼ cups milk or plant-based milk
- 50 g/3½ tablespoons Greek or plant-based yogurt
- 1 tablespoon runny honey or maple syrup
- ½ teaspoon ground cinnamon or ground ginger
- 65 g/scant ⅓ cup smooth peanut butter

Directions:

1. Stir all the ingredients together in a bowl, then transfer to a baking dish that fits your air-fryer drawer.
2. Preheat the air-fryer to 180°C/350°F.
3. Add the baking dish to the preheated air-fryer and air-fry for 10 minutes. Remove from the air-fryer and serve hot, cut into 9 squares.

Chonut Holes

Servings: 12
Cooking Time: xx

Ingredients:

- 225g flour
- 75g sugar
- 1 tsp baking powder
- ¼ tsp cinnamon
- 2 tbsp sugar
- ½ tsp salt
- 2 tbsp aquafaba
- 1 tbsp melted coconut oil
- 75ml soy milk
- 2 tsp cinnamon

Directions:

1. In a bowl mix the flour, ¼ cup sugar, baking powder, ¼ tsp cinnamon and salt
2. Add the aquafaba, coconut oil and soy milk mix well
3. In another bowl mix 2 tsp cinnamon and 2 tbsp sugar
4. Line the air fryer with parchment paper
5. Divide the dough into 12 pieces and dredge with the cinnamon sugar mix
6. Place in the air fryer at 185°C and cook for 6-8 minutes, don't shake them

Apple And Cinnamon Puff Pastry Pies

Servings:8
Cooking Time:20 Minutes
Ingredients:
- 4 tbsp butter
- 4 tbsp white sugar
- 2 tbsp brown sugar
- 1 tsp cinnamon
- 1 tsp nutmeg
- 1 tsp salt
- 4 apples, peeled and diced
- 2 large sheets puff pastry
- 1 egg

Directions:
1. Preheat the air fryer to 180 °C / 350 °F. Remove the mesh basket from the machine and line it with parchment paper.
2. In a bowl, whisk together the butter, white sugar, brown sugar, cinnamon, nutmeg, and salt.
3. Place the apples in a heatproof baking dish and coat them in the butter and sugar mixture. Transfer to the air fryer and cook for 10 minutes.
4. Meanwhile, roll out the pastry on a clean, floured surface. Cut the sheets into 8 equal parts.
5. Once the apples are hot and softened, evenly spread the mixture between the pastry sheets. Fold the sheets over to cover the apple and gently press the edges using a fork or your fingers to seal the mixture in.
6. Beat the egg in a bowl and use a brush to coat the top of each pastry sheet.
7. Carefully transfer the filled pastry sheets to the prepared air fryer basket, close the lid, and cook for 10 minutes until the pastry is golden and crispy.

Banana And Nutella Sandwich

Servings: 2
Cooking Time:xx
Ingredients:
- Softened butter
- 4 slices white bread
- 25g chocolate spread
- 1 banana

Directions:
1. Preheat the air fryer to 185°C
2. Spread butter on one side of all the bread slices
3. Spread chocolate spread on the other side of each slice
4. Add sliced banana to two slices of bread then add the other slice of bread to each
5. Cut in half diagonally to form triangles
6. Place in the air fryer and cook for 5 minutes turn over and cook for another 2 minutes

Pistachio Brownies

Servings: 4
Cooking Time:xx
Ingredients:
- 75ml milk
- ½ tsp vanilla extract
- 25g salt
- 25g pecans
- 75g flour
- 75g sugar
- 25g cocoa powder
- 1 tbsp ground flax seeds

Directions:
1. Mix all of the dry ingredients together, in another bowl mix the wet ingredients
2. Add all the ingredients together and mix well
3. Preheat the air fryer to 175°C
4. Line a 5 inch cake tin with parchment paper
5. Pour the brownie mix into the cake tin and cook in the air fryer for about 20 minutes

New York Cheesecake

Servings: 8
Cooking Time:xx
Ingredients:
- 225g plain flour
- 100g brown sugar
- 100g butter
- 50g melted butter
- 1 tbsp vanilla essence
- 750g soft cheese
- 2 cups caster sugar
- 3 large eggs
- 50ml quark

Directions:
1. Add the flour, sugar, and 100g butter to a bowl and mix until combined. Form into biscuit shapes place in the air fryer and cook for 15 minutes at 180°C
2. Grease a springform tin
3. Break the biscuits up and mix with the melted butter, press firmly into the tin
4. Mix the soft cheese and sugar in a bowl until creamy, add the eggs and vanilla and mix. Mix in the quark
5. Pour the cheesecake batter into the pan
6. Place in your air fryer and cook for 30 minutes at 180°C. Leave in the air fryer for 30 minutes whilst it cools
7. Refrigerate for 6 hours

Milk And White Chocolate Chip Air Fryer Donuts With Frosting

Servings:4
Cooking Time:10 Minutes

Ingredients:
- For the donuts:
- 200 ml milk (any kind)
- 50 g / 3.5 oz brown sugar
- 50 g / 3.5 oz granulated sugar
- 1 tbsp active dry yeast
- 2 tbsp olive oil
- 4 tbsp butter, melted
- 1 egg, beaten
- 1 tsp vanilla extract
- 400 g / 14 oz plain flour
- 4 tbsp cocoa powder
- 100 g / 3.5 oz milk chocolate chips
- For the frosting:
- 5 tbsp powdered sugar
- 2 tbsp cocoa powder
- 100 ml heavy cream
- 50 g / 1.8 oz white chocolate chips, melted

Directions:
1. To make the donuts, whisk together the milk, brown and granulated sugars, and active dry yeast in a bowl. Set aside for a few minutes while the yeast starts to get foamy.
2. Stir the melted butter, beaten egg, and vanilla extract into the bowl. Mix well until all of the ingredients are combined.
3. Fold in the plain flour and cocoa powder until a smooth mixture forms.
4. Lightly flour a clean kitchen top surface and roll the dough out. Gently knead the dough for 2-3 minutes until it becomes soft and slightly tacky.
5. Transfer the dough into a large mixing bowl and cover it with a clean tea towel or some tinfoil. Leave the dough to rise for around one hour in a warm place.
6. Remove the tea towel or tinfoil from the bowl and roll it out on a floured surface once again. Use a rolling pin to roll the dough into a one-inch thick circle.
7. Use a round cookie cutter to create circular donuts and place each one into a lined air fryer basket.
8. Once all of the donuts have been placed into the air fryer, turn the machine onto 150 °C / 300 °F and close the lid.
9. Cook the donuts for 8-10 minutes until they are slightly golden and crispy on the outside.
10. While the donuts are cooking in the air fryer, make the frosting by combining the powdered sugar, cocoa powder, heavy cream, and melted white chocolate chips in a bowl. Mix well until a smooth, sticky mixture forms.
11. When the donuts are cooked, remove them from the air fryer and set aside to cool for 5-10 minutes. Once cooled, evenly spread some frosting on the top layer of each one. Place in the fridge to set for at least one hour.
12. Enjoy the donuts hot or cold.

Pop Tarts

Servings: 6
Cooking Time:xx

Ingredients:
- 200g strawberries quartered
- 25g sugar
- ½ pack ready made pie crust
- Cooking spray
- 50g powdered sugar
- 1 ½ tsp lemon juice
- 1 tbsp sprinkles

Directions:
1. Stir together strawberries and sugar in a bowl
2. Allow to stand for 15 minutes then microwave on high for 10 minutes stirring halfway through
3. Roll out pie crust into 12 inch circle, cut into 12 rectangles
4. Spoon mix onto 6 of the rectangles
5. Brush the edges with water and top with the remaining rectangles
6. Press around the edges with a fork to seal
7. Place in the air fryer and cook at 175°C for about 10 minutes
8. Mix together powdered sugar and decorate add sprinkles

Banana Bread

Servings: 8
Cooking Time:xx

Ingredients:
- 200g flour
- 1 tsp cinnamon
- ½ tsp salt
- ¼ tsp baking soda
- 2 ripe banana mashed
- 2 large eggs
- 75g sugar
- 25g plain yogurt
- 2 tbsp oil
- 1 tsp vanilla extract
- 2 tbsp chopped walnuts
- Cooking spray

Directions:
1. Line a 6 inch cake tin with parchment paper and coat with cooking spray
2. Whisk together flour, cinnamon, salt and baking soda set aside
3. In another bowl mix together remaining ingredients, add the flour mix and combine well
4. Pour batter into the cake tin and place in the air fryer
5. Cook at 155°C for 35 minutes turning halfway through

Banana Cake

Servings: 4
Cooking Time:xx
Ingredients:
- Cooking spray
- 25g brown sugar
- ½ tbsp butter
- 1 banana, mashed
- 1 egg
- 2 tbsp honey
- 225g self raising flour
- ½ tsp cinnamon
- Pinch salt

Directions:
1. Preheat air fryer to 160°C
2. Spray a small fluted tube tray with cooking spray
3. Beat sugar and butter together in a bowl until creamy
4. Combine the banana egg and honey together in another bowl
5. Mix into the butter until smooth
6. Sift in the remaining ingredients and mix well
7. Spoon into the tray and cook in the air fryer for 30 minutes

Butter Cake

Servings: 4
Cooking Time:xx
Ingredients:
- Cooking spray
- 7 tbsp butter
- 25g white sugar
- 2 tbsp white sugar
- 1 egg
- 300g flour
- Pinch salt
- 6 tbsp milk

Directions:
1. Preheat air fryer to 175°C
2. Spray a small fluted tube pan with cooking spray
3. Beat the butter and all of the sugar together in a bowl until creamy
4. Add the egg and mix until fluffy, add the salt and flour mix well. Add the milk and mix well
5. Put the mix in the pan and cook in the air fryer for 15 minutes

Breakfast Muffins

Servings:4
Cooking Time:xx
Ingredients:

- 1 eating apple, cored and grated
- 40 g/2 heaped tablespoons maple syrup
- 40 ml/3 tablespoons oil (avocado, olive or coconut), plus extra for greasing
- 1 egg
- 40 ml/3 tablespoons milk (plant-based if you wish)
- 90 g/scant ¾ cup brown rice flour
- 50 g/½ cup ground almonds
- ¾ teaspoon ground cinnamon
- ⅛ teaspoon ground cloves
- ¼ teaspoon salt
- 1 teaspoon baking powder
- Greek or plant-based yogurt and fresh fruit, to serve

Directions:

1. In a bowl mix the grated apple, maple syrup, oil, egg and milk. In another bowl mix the rice flour, ground almonds, cinnamon, cloves, salt and baking powder. Combine the wet ingredients with the dry, mixing until there are no visible patches of the flour mixture left. Grease 4 ramekins and divide the batter equally between them.
2. Preheat the air-fryer to 160°C/325°F.
3. Add the ramekins to the preheated air-fryer and air-fry for 12 minutes. Check the muffins are cooked by inserting a cocktail stick/toothpick into the middle of one of the muffins. If it comes out clean, the muffins are ready; if not, cook for a further couple of minutes.
4. Allow to cool in the ramekins, then remove and serve with your choice of yogurt and fresh fruit.

White Chocolate Pudding

Servings:2
Cooking Time:15 Minutes
Ingredients:

- 100 g / 3.5 oz white chocolate
- 50 g brown sugar
- 2 tbsp olive oil
- ½ tsp vanilla extract
- 4 egg whites, plus two egg yolks

Directions:

1. Preheat the air fryer to 180 °C / 350 °F and line the mesh basket with parchment paper or grease it with olive oil.
2. Place the white chocolate in a saucepan and place it over low heat until it melts, being careful not to let the chocolate burn.
3. Stir in the brown sugar, olive oil, and vanilla extract.
4. Whisk the egg whites and egg yolks in a bowl until well combined. Fold a third of the eggs into the white chocolate mixture and stir until it forms a smooth and consistent mixture. Repeat twice more with the other two-thirds of the eggs.
5. Pour the white chocolate pudding mixture evenly into two ramekins and place the ramekins in the lined air fryer basket. Cook for 15 minutes until the pudding is hot and set on top.

RECIPES INDEX

A

Air Fried Maple Chicken Thighs 66

Air Fried Scallops 69

Air Fryer Bbq Chicken 57

Air Fryer Chicken Thigh Schnitzel 57

Air Fryer Eggy Bread 91

Air Fryer Mussels 78

Air-fried Artichoke Hearts 39

Air-fried Pickles 32

Alternative Stuffed Potatoes 90

Apple And Cinnamon Puff Pastry Pies 98

Apple Crisps 12

Artichoke Pasta 35

Asparagus Spears 85

Aubergine Parmesan 82

B

Baba Ganoush 17

Banana And Nutella Sandwich 98

Banana Bread 101

Banana Cake 102

Beef Kebobs 46

Blanket Breakfast Eggs 20

Bocconcini Balls 11

Brazilian Pineapple 94

Breaded Pork Chops 55

Breakfast Eggs & Spinach 15

Breakfast Muffins 103

Breakfast Sausage Burgers 10

Buffalo Wings 67

Butter Cake 102

Buttermilk Pork Chops 49

Butternut Squash Fries 85

C

Cajun Prawn Skewers 78

Cajun Shrimp Boil 70

Carne Asada Chips 50

Cauliflower With Hot Sauce And Blue Cheese Sauce 87

Celery Root Fries 86

Cheddar & Bbq Stuffed Chicken 60

Cheese Wontons 24

Cheesy Garlic Asparagus 81

Cheesy Taco Crescents 28

Chicken & Bacon Parcels 30

Chicken & Potatoes 58

Chicken And Wheat Stir Fry 59

Chicken Jalfrezi 67

Chicken Kiev 65

Chicken Milanese 64

Chicken Parmesan With Marinara Sauce 61

Chicken Tikka Masala 64

Chilli Lime Tilapia 76

Chinese Chilli Beef 56

Chocolate Cake 95

Chocolate Mug Cake 94

Chonut Holes 97

Cinnamon Biscuit Bites 93

Cinnamon-maple Pineapple Kebabs 93

Cod Nuggets 79

Copycat Fish Fingers 69

Corn Nuts 28

Cornflake Chicken Nuggets 66

Courgette Burgers 37

Crispy Broccoli 89

Crispy Cinnamon French Toast 91

Crispy Cornish Hen 60

Crispy Sweet & Spicy Cauliflower 88

Crunchy Fish 79

Crunchy Mexican Breakfast Wrap 13

E

Easy Cheesy Scrambled Eggs 11

Easy Omelette 19

Egg & Bacon Breakfast Cups 17

European Pancakes 15

Extra Crispy Popcorn Shrimp 72

F

Fish In Foil 70

Fish In Parchment Paper 72

Fish Taco Cauliflower Rice Bowls 74

French Toast 16

French Toast Slices 21

G

Garlic Tilapia 76

German Rouladen 52

Gluten Free Honey And Garlic Shrimp 75

Gnocchi Caprese 41

Goat's Cheese Tartlets 44

Grilled Ginger & Coconut Pineapple Rings 96

H

Hamburgers With Feta 49

Hard Boiled Eggs Air Fryer Style 12

Healthy Breakfast Bagels 14

Healthy Stuffed Peppers 18

Honey & Mustard Meatballs 53

Honey Roasted Parsnips 87

Honey Sriracha Salmon 77

I

Italian Meatballs 53

Italian Rice Balls 22

J

Jackfruit Taquitos 38

Jalapeño Poppers 24

L

Lamb Burgers 51

Lentil Burgers 42

M

Mac & Cheese Bites 29

Macaroni & Cheese Quiche 41

Mahi Fish Tacos 71

Meatballs In Tomato Sauce 54

Meaty Egg Cups 16

Mediterranean Vegetables 90

Mexican Breakfast Burritos 10

Milk And White Chocolate Chip Air Fryer Donuts With Frosting 100

Mini Quiche 43

Mongolian Beef 47

Mozzarella Sticks 25

N

Nashville Chicken 63

New York Cheesecake 99

O

Onion Dumplings 36

Onion Pakoda 27

Oozing Baked Eggs 20

Orange Sesame Cauliflower 86

Orange Tofu 83

P

Paneer Tikka 45

Parmesan-coated Fish Fingers 71

Pasta Chips 29

Peach Pies(1) 96

Peanut Butter & Chocolate Baked Oats 97

Pepper & Lemon Chicken Wings 58

Pepperoni Bread 25

Peppers With Aioli Dip 23

Pistachio Brownies 99

Pizza Chicken Nuggets 68

Polenta Fries 18

Pop Tarts 101

Popcorn Tofu 33

Pork Schnitzel 48

Pork Taquitos 54

Potato Fries 14

Potato Gratin 38

Potato Wedges 84

Potato Wedges With Rosemary 81

Pretzel Bites 31

Pulled Pork, Bacon, And Cheese Sliders 55

Q

Quick Chicken Nuggets 65

R

Rainbow Vegetables 37

Ranch Style Fish Fillets 77

Ratatouille 35

Ricotta Stuffed Aubergine 89

Roast Beef 52

Roast Vegetables 36

S

Saganaki 42

Salt & Pepper Calamari 74

Salt And Pepper Belly Pork 52

Salt And Vinegar Chickpeas 31

Satay Chicken Skewers 68

Shakshuka 40

Shishito Peppers 84

Shrimp With Yum Yum Sauce 73

Smoky Chicken Breast 62

Snack Style Falafel 30

Spicy Chicken Wing Drummettes 62

Spicy Chickpeas 27

Spicy Peanuts 23

Spinach And Feta Croissants 45

Spring Ratatouille 39

Steak And Mushrooms 47

Steak Dinner 51

Steak Fajitas 50

Sticky Tofu With Cauliflower Rice 34

Store-cupboard Fishcakes 75

Strawberry Danish 92

Stuffed Mushrooms 26

Super Easy Fries 83

Sweet And Sticky Ribs 46

T

Tahini Beef Bites 48

Tasty Pumpkin Seeds 26

Thai Fish Cakes 73

Thai Fried Bananas 92

Thai-style Tuna Fishcakes 80

Toad In The Hole, Breakfast Style 13

Turkey And Mushroom Burgers 61

Turkey Cutlets In Mushroom Sauce 59

V

Vegan Meatballs 44

Vegetable & Beef Frittata 56

Veggie Bakes 43

W

Waffle Fries 32

weet Potato Crisps 29

White Chocolate And Raspberry Loaf 95

White Chocolate Pudding 103

Whole Sweet Potatoes 88

Whole Wheat Pizza 34

Wholegrain Pitta Chips 19

Y

Yorkshire Puddings 82

Z

Zingy Roasted Carrots 85

Printed in Great Britain
by Amazon